D0824755

Association Football

Match Control

Also by Stanley F. Lover:
Association Football Laws Illustrated

Association Football Match Control

AN ILLUSTRATED HANDBOOK
FOR THE
FOOTBALL REFEREE .

BY STANLEY F. LOVER

FOREWORD BY
SIR STANLEY ROUS CBE

PELHAM BOOKS
LONDON

First published in Great Britain by
Pelham Books Ltd
52 Bedford Square
London WC1

1978

© 1978 by Stanley F. Lover

ISBN 0 7207 1035 9

Set in 11/13 Plantin by Saildean Limited, Kingston.
Printed in Great Britain
by Hollen Street Press at Slough

Contents

Foreword

This book is a comprehensive study of every aspect of refereeing, but should appeal also to players, officials and supporters. There is much in it to interest everybody connected in any way with the game.

I have known the author for many years, during which he has accomplished much to improve the standard of Association Football referees by writing, lecturing and producing instructional films. Since he retired after twenty-five years in active refereeing Stan Lover has devoted much time to lecturing at courses on behalf of FIFA and the FA in Australia, New Zealand, South Africa, Holland, Northern Ireland and in many other footballing countries which have invited him to conduct courses or present special talks in his capacity as a FIFA lecturer. The British Council also invited him to undertake a lecture tour to Nigeria.

In this country he has given talks and led seminars and practical demonstrations at scores of referee societies. He is a past president of the Football League Referees' and Linesmen's Association and is president of LONSAR, the London Referees' Society having been its chairman for nine years. He is therefore experienced and well qualified to write a book which will appeal to referees, from the 'recruit' stage through junior and senior to international level. Everyone will find something of value in this work. It is a historical, educational textbook which will stimulate referees to think about their problems and realize their vital role in the game. Chapters 4, 8 and 10 are especially designed to that end. That are many original ideas and viewpoints which will provide referee instructors with suitable material for their talks to fellow referees.

The carefully selected illustrations add greatly to the value of the book and the sketches of match incidents in chapter 13 are most instructive.

I hope that this book will be widely read, but it must not be read once and put on a shelf. Referees should use it as a ready reference book. Its great value for them will be as a means of refreshing and reminding themselves of their responsibility to the game throughout their career. It is an excellent complementary work to the author's first book, *Association Football Laws Illustrated*, which has become an established textbook throughout world football. Together these publications provide a comprehensive analysis of the laws and their practical application.

Finally, this book provides an opportunity for all who are interested in Association Football to increase their knowledge of and to obtain more pleasure from the most popular game in the world – soccer.

Stanley Rous,
Honorary President of FIFA
August 1977

Introduction

There was a time when the soccer referee needed only a sound knowledge of the laws, strong lungs to blow a whistle and a pair of reasonably active legs to control a football match. Some, who lacked one or more of these essentials, were able to get by with the aid of a forceful personality.

Today's referee, and tomorrow's, needs something extra. He needs to understand the reasons why he wants to referee. He needs deeper knowledge of the game, its players, their skills, the styles and tactics of team play, and the physical and mental pressures which arise in competitive situations. He needs to develop good technique in man-management, to know about gamesmanship ploys, the latest thinking in law changes and the problems which have given rise to such changes. He needs to study the influences of various factors on match control which, in the past, have tended to be only of passing interest.

Demands on fitness and mobility have increased with the changing tempo of modern football. Demands on personal time and dedication have increased with the need to assimilate an accelerating flow of information and instructions. The modern referee needs much more help and guidance than his predecessors and he needs both much earlier in his career.

To be able to contribute his best to the game he needs individual tuition on the techniques of practical match control which take into account his own character, personality and ability. He should be given expert advice on personal grooming for his role as a representative of the football authority he serves. He needs access to regular and progressively structured refresher courses including medical and physical tests. These are the basic elements of the preparation and monitoring of the future match official.

The foregoing observations are a summary of opinions expressed by many referees at meetings and courses in various countries. They represent also the views of others in the game who are concerned with improving the standard of match control. Many officials are ready and willing to undertake the additional effort involved and seek active encouragement from football authority.

With all this in mind this work has been prepared to advise on match control techniques and to provide a framework within which each individual can develop his understanding and knowledge to improve personal performance on the field of play.

Several references to top levels of soccer are included because football at all levels is influenced by what is seen in televised matches and discussed on radio or in the press. In addition the football world is becoming smaller as new means are found to move teams between nations and continents, not only at international and professional club level but at all levels.

The first FIFA (Fédération Internationale de Football Association) World Youth Tournament, successfully completed in Tunisia in 1977, was indicative of the widening exchange of young footballers. Sponsored weekend visits by teams of schoolboys between Australia and Europe, using Concorde, are already being planned. World league type competitions at schoolboy and youth level may not be too far away.

For the football referee there are exciting possibilities ahead – much to plan for and prepare. It is the object of this book to assist the modern referee in successfully tackling the problems which will be confronted. It has been prepared with the invaluable assistance and advice of many people. Grateful acknowledgement is extended to FIFA and The Football Association for permission to reproduce or quote from authoritative material; to the editor and staff of the IPC Magazine *Shoot* for permission to include illustrated match incidents in chapter 13 and Styx cartoons; to the Arsenal Football Club for the excellent Heath cartoon; to the London Football Association and to a long list of individuals who have contributed material, comments, typing expertise and reproduction facilities.

Stanley F. Lover

1 Football and you

What does *football* mean to you? Are you attracted to the game by a simple interest in an athletic activity; as a means of self-expression; for involvement and companionship, or, perhaps by some inexplicable passion? The value of this book will depend to a large extent on your answer to the question. Before entering into the theory and practice of match control, it will be helpful to establish what your feelings are about the game. This opening chapter is intended to initiate personal reflection on aspects of the game which may have influenced your decision to take an interest in serving football as a match official.

But first, what is football? What are the virtues which have made the game the most popular sport in the world? Dictionary definitions are not helpful in pointing the way towards the magnetism of the game, as the following examples illustrate: 1) 'football ... large, round, inflated ball; a game played with it' (*Oxford Dictionary*) and 2) 'football ... open-air game played with a ball by two sides, each trying to kick it over the other's goal-line' (*Modern English Dictionary*) These and other definitions can only describe football as an object or the basic mechanics of playing the game.

Many enthusiasts are no doubt attracted to the game by the pleasures of healthy exercise. An interesting description of this aspect of football was written by Richard Mulcaster, the headmaster of Merchant Taylors' and St Paul's schools in 1581. He was a deep-thinking advocate of football and he proposed several constructive ideas some of which did not gain acceptance until the nineteenth century:

> Football strengtheneth and brawneth the whole body and, by provoking superfluities downward, it dischargeth the head and upper parts. It is good for the bowels and to drive down the stone and gravell from both the bladder and the kidneys.
>
> It helpeth weak hammes, by much moving, beginning at the meane and simple shankes by thickening of the fleshe no less than riding doth. Yet rash running and too much force oftentime breaketh some inward conduit and brineth ruptures.

There is a large element of truth in these observations, but hardly enough to explain the universal acceptance of football as a major leisure-time activity. Views on the game vary from this somewhat basic description to an all-embracing philosophical concept which introoduces moral values and higher human qualities.

One of the game's attractions is its simplicity. It is also an emotional experience. It has an unspoken world language and the power to concentrate the attention of a large proportion of the world's population on a peaceful pastime. People of all ages, sexes and nationalities and with diametrically opposed religious, political and philosophical views, have discovered that the sport provides an exciting and yet relaxing therapy for life's daily problems. It could be argued with some justification that it is more widely practised and discussed than love, the basic emotion of life. It certain involves more than one emotion, as any independent observer can see by studying the reactions of those who play in, and those who watch, just one match. Every emotion, with its full range of expression, emerges during the uncertain ebb and flow of a contest between two great teams struggling for supremacy, engaged in a sporting battle for fame and fortune.

Perhaps many readers are attracted to the sport by the skills of individuals, and have experienced moments of tingling excitement as masters of the game perform magical feats of control over body and ball or at the breathtaking power of a swift shot at goal. Masters like Pelé of Brazil, Cruyff of Holland, Beckenbauer of West Germany, in the modern era; Bobby Charlton of England, Puskas of Hungary, Eusebio of Portugal, Yashin of the USSR, in the recent past; and reaching further into football history, Stanley Matthews, Alex James, Ted Drake, Frank Swift, Tommy Walker, Dixie Dean, Hughie Gallacher and the early outstanding amateurs. These last include characters like Lord Kinnaird, who contrasted a flowing red beard with cricket cap, flannels and shirt. Such players, and many more, have become legendary figures in football folklore and will stir nostalgia in those who have followed football for many years. Most of the names are better known than many politicians who have successfully fashioned great economies or generals who have led great armies. The names of great footballers certainly come more readily to the lips of young football enthusiasts.

Passions for football often begin at an early age and last a lifetime. It is easy to understand how a child will catch football fever if he or she lives in the hotbed environment of a football-crazy household or in a locality sporting a famous team. Perhaps this was your particular nursery. No risk to life or limb is too great to some full-blooded football devotees in order to be part of the mass of humanity at an important match and to be engulfed in rapidly rising or falling waves of emotion which sweep across the playing arena.

Football has been described as an escape route for feelings unexpressed outside the football stadium. There is much truth in this. During just a few minutes of play many uninhibited facial expressions and body movements will be displayed which would not be seen, even by a patient observer, during weeks of 'normal' public life. It can seem then that the simple game of football is a means of expressing a range of emotions which few or no other activities can touch. The therapeutic value of the sport is described in the following story, written by a young engineer after a visit to West Africa:

We had stopped for petrol. It was hot. The West African sun blazed into the tiny car and I felt uncomfortable from the remains of a fever which had left me weak after a hurried vaccination had gone wrong. Kurt, my companion, was busy with the attendant discussing quantity and price at the sole, sad-looking pump which must have been the original model designed when petrol was discovered. It looked as I felt – sick. In need of a rest, a coat of paint, elbow grease on parts meant to be bright and cheerful but now covered with grime and brick-red dust from the bush road. My mouth was dry, my body beginning to burn from the heat, from the fever. Thin cotton shirt, white tropical shorts and open sandals were all that I wore. But I perspired.

We had only just started our journey on the road from Accra to the Volta Dam. This was supposed to be the cool of the morning. The worst was yet to come. Could I last out the whole day? Could I now suggest that we postpone the visit? Would Kurt agree to take me back to my bungalow where I had a stock of cold drinks and a large fan which swished lazily, but efficiently and coolly, over my bed. I could rest there all day and be fit for the journey tomorrow. But, no, it would cause too many complications.

I left the car and walked towards the nearest available shade, by the wall of a small one-storey building which served as the house, office and storeroom of the petrol-station attendant. He was now talking animatedly to Kurt, his wide hat flopping up and down rhythmically with the movement of his head as he made his point.

Approaching the house I became aware of noise and movement on the balcony which jutted out over the entrance. What I saw attracted my interest. Two small boys, no more than seven or eight years of age, moved excitedly and happily on an area about three metres long by two metres wide. They were playing football. They were not aware of my presence as I watched. They were in a world of their own. Poorly clothed, with thin bodies, their faces however carried a constant broad smile and displayed gleaming white teeth when their wide mouths broke into laughter.

Apart from their restricted pitch the only accessory was a ball - a tight bundle of rags. No goalposts, corner flags, referee or linesman, but in their imagination they played out the most important match in the world. They wriggled and jumped, kicked and pushed with the wild excitement of free expression. One boy picked up the ball by gripping his toes on a stray end of rag. This caused both to burst into great shrieks of laughter and giggles. A joy to watch. I was transported into another world for what seemed an age, and yet it proved to be only a few minutes.

In their world they were the great Pelé or another soccer idol, bobbing, weaving, beating formidable opponents with a body swerve, a drag-back, swift acceleration and scoring the winning goal in the World Cup Final with a brilliantly judged volley which crashed into the back of the net. In reality the rag ball came spinning down and landed in a puff of red dust at my feet. Two excited faces looked down, silently imploring me to throw back their ball. I did. The ball had hardly touched the balcony before a new World Cup Final began amid shouts, laughs and giggles in complete isolation from that other world of reality.

Those few moments gave me great joy and elation. My cares were forgotten. 'Are you coming?' cried Kurt. I returned to the car feeling refreshed after that invigorating journey into another world: the magic world of football.

There can be no doubt what the author's own feelings were about the game. He later explained that he was unaware of these feelings until he had observed their expression through the medium of two small boys. Perhaps you can relate to a similar experience.

Football fever is not always caught at an early age, as has been seen in the past ten years in the growing popularity of the game in the United States of America. Many American adults, who have only recently been converted to the 'round ball' version of football, will not have experienced the childhood pleasures just described. Maybe, as lovers of sport, they relate to early experiences of other sporting activities and see in football equivalent or more satisfying pleasures for themselves and for their children. The game is attracting many more women, some as players, a few as referees, but many as spectators. These newcomers to the sport will ensure its enthusiastic continuation, for they are the mothers of current and future generations of football players. In future studies of our civilization football should be rated as a major twentieth-century social phenomenon. It is a sobering thought that more people on this earth watched the 1974 World Cup series taking place in

Germany than watched the first moon-landing. On reflection, this may not be so surprising because one is real and tangible, the other remote and bordering on the realms of fantasy.

Simple as the game is, football has its own subtle ingredients of mystery, suspense, drama and pathos, special qualities of spontaneous humour which bring life and brightness to many a dull heart. Is this what football means to you? Or are you attracted by its colour, speed, athletic grace and power? Perhaps your personal interest has already been expressed in some, or even all, of the foregoing comments. Whatever your motives for becoming involved in the game, whether as a player, coach, administrator or referee, there is no doubt that your actions both on and off the field will truthfully reflect your inner feelings for the sport. While this work is designed to assist in the efficient and fair control of the playing of the game it may also serve as a commentary on the attitudes of those who take part.

To have made the decision to accept the role of arbitrator is to declare your personal commitment to the game. As an observer you will have seen that such a role is neither popular nor glamorous. But it is respected by those who share your concern that the principles and reputation of the sport must be preserved. You will be joining, or have already joined, a relatively small band of individuals who are prepared to withstand criticism and apply unselfish devotion to ensure that the pleasures of the game are available for those who seek them. Your success in achieving this objective will be your reward. Newcomers to the role of match official should be in no doubt that the task ahead will be difficult. Dedication will be tested on many occasions and in many ways.

In recent times demands on match officials have become more pressing as the competitive element has intensified. Skills, methods of play and tactics become ever more sophisticated. To keep abreast of new ideas, qualities additional to those which have always applied to the referee, such as courage, integrity and determination, are needed in the current and future era of officials. It is important for the referee to be knowledgeable about some aspects of the game which have hitherto been of only passing interest or have been picked up piecemeal over the course of years. Deeper awareness of the influences of physical and psychological factors, development of techniques in reading situations, knowledge of latest tactical innovations, constant reappraisal of fundamental principles and personal analysis are but some of the widening areas for study. There is more to match control than an expert knowledge of the written laws of the game, as the following chapters will attempt to demonstrate.

This chapter tries to help crystallize your personal understanding and inner feelings about the game. If there remain any areas of doubt it is hoped that in the following pages you will find pieces of the jigsaw which, when brought together at the end, will present a clear picture and point the way to the successful planning of your future career as a referee.

Is there such a person as a typical referee? If there is, what qualities distinguish him from others? A recent survey of Football League referees produced the following cross-section of occupations:

factory managers	19
teachers and lecturers	13
engineers	11
salesmen	11
tradesmen	10
company directors	8
civil servants	8
accountants	7
shopkeepeers	5

The remainder included four in police work, a finger-print expert, bricklayer, soldier, docker, farmer and the best known of them all, a master butcher, Jack Taylor. Common links between these varied occupations are that all involve some degree of formal training, personal application and responsibility. Nearly all require good relationships with other people, whether in a business or an educational capacity.

The ability to communicate successfully with others is nearly always an important career requirement. Experience of life, maturity and integrity are essential to most successful careers. From my observation, referees at this level show a dignified and confident manner in their dealings with colleagues and administrators within the game. The list of common factors among referees who have reached a high level in football looks formidable:

1	formal training	6	experience
2	personal application	7	maturity
3	responsibility	8	integrity
4	good relationships	9	dignified bearing
5	good communication	10	confidence

These are the successful officials. All have served their apprenticeship in junior football. Many continue to officiate at junior level when not engaged in professional matches. A few (seven per country) are accepted onto the FIFA list of international referees and are required to add diplomacy to the qualities already listed. To be chosen as one of some thirty referees to take part in the final stages of the World Cup is a rare honour. The chosen few for the 1974 tournament were selected from twenty-eight different countries and their preparation for that event is described by Ken Aston in chapter 11. The complete list, together with personal details and photographs, appears in the appendix. As in the case of the Football League survey, occupations are varied, but the qualities needed are the same. One additional factor is that two thirds are able to communicate in a foreign language as well as their own.

These comments have concentrated on the men at the top, but they can be applied to all levels. If there are any heroes in the game they must surely include the thousands of referees who have faint chance to reach the top. Men (and women) who are content to devote a large slice of their lives to the service of the game at junior level contribute much to the community.

2 The Spirit of the Game

Football, as we have seen in the previous chapter, generates intense emotions. Wherever the game is played its strengths, its weaknesses, and its myriad fascinations are debated. It must be true that as much emotion is generated away from the football field as on it.

This is particularly true in the world of the match official who engages in debate with colleagues on aspects of the laws of the game. At such gatherings it is not uncommon for just one word of football law to be the subject of long and minute examination to determine its true meaning and interpretation. Frequently the debate ends with the question unresolved. Attempts are made to obtain definitive rulings from higher authority, from regional or national referees' organizations, from the national football association or, ultimately, from world authorities responsible for law-making, namely FIFA and the International Football Association Board.

Sometimes thirty to forty referees, some of them very experienced, discuss a hypothetical question such as: 'You have awarded a penalty kick. When the ball is kicked it strikes the crossbar and bursts. The inner casing goes into the goal and the outer casing goes over the crossbar. What is the correct decision?' The odds against an incident such as this occurring during the career of an individual referee are astronomical; it is certainly not worth thirty to forty man hours of unfruitful discussion. And even more certainly, it would not be worth troubling busy administrators with requests for written answers to this and to many similar hypothetical situations. On the other hand some serious problems have arisen which have required clarification. Also, trends in playing the game, such as too much emphasis on defensive tactics or abuse of the off-side law, have invoked appeals to make alterations to keep the game as attractive as possible.

During discussions on law problems a vital factor is often overlooked. This factor was spelt out by the International Board in a statement issued in Dubrovnik in 1968 after its annual meeting to review the laws. It read:

> The International Football Association Board received many suggestions for improving the game and alterations to the laws, and such suggestions were carefully studied. It is the belief of the Board, however, that the spirit in which the game is played is of paramount importance and that changes in the laws to improve the game as a spectacle are of little value if 'fair play' is not universally observed.

'The spirit of the game is of paramount importance.' Words of wisdom, worthy of repetition. An appeal to keep the 'spirit' above all other considerations cannot be ignored. It is an appeal to all who take part in football whether as players, coaches, match officials or as administrators.

What is the special significance of this appeal to the referee? What is *his* role in its interpretation and application? What is meant by 'the spirit of the game'? If it is so important it should be clearly understood by all so that we work together from a common base.

In 1957 the International Board gave guiding counsel. It commented on the differing practices which had appeared in countries where football had developed along paths that diverged from the code of conduct established in the early days of the game in Britain. For football to exist as a world game it became essential to move towards a common interpretation of such practices as deliberate obstruction, handling the ball to prevent a vital movement of play, time-wasting tactics, dissent, and other acts which provoked different reactions according to national traditions and temperaments. A clue to the meaning of 'the spirit of the game' appeared in an introduction to a few of the practices needing review:

> The laws of the game and the rulings of the International Board and FIFA cannot of themselves bring about the exemplary code of behaviour which is so often referred to as 'the spirit of the game'. If football is to continue to be one of the great and most popular games in the world then those who take part in it must keep up its great tradition. Everyone wishes to win but true sportsmen can find small satisfaction in a victory won by unfair means. The spirit of the law must be observed as well as the letter of the law.

The last sentence indicates the role of the referee in safeguarding the spirit of the game, for it is clear that, apart from understanding the written law, he must understand the spirit behind the law.

How can we identify the spirit in the laws? Is it some misty intangible aura which surrounds those thousands of dry and dusty words which form the seventeen laws of the game? Or is it something that can be defined in such a way that these same words become vital, alive, meaningful – signposts to the heart of the game? Match officials both new and experienced need guidance in identifying the basic elements, to enable them to sharpen their own attitudes in the practical application of the written law.

Where do we look to find the spirit, the lifeblood of the heart of football? It will help if we look back for a moment at the beginnings of the modern game and analyse the basic principles adopted when football became organized: the principles which were locked into the first laws by the founders of what has become such a pleasurable pastime for millions. A simple key can unlock these principles from the laws, showing how they are implanted in those many cold legalistic phrases, giving to the bare bones of everyday words the flesh and muscle, energy and vitality, that we see on the field of play. In chapters which follow we will see the practical application of the spirit in playing situations.

The method of play

The most significant milestone in football history occurred in 1863 when The Football Association was born. Until then there had been no universal code for the conduct of play in a game which had historical references stretching back over two thousand years. Several excellent works have been compiled on the historical development of the game. Some are listed in the bibliography at the end of this book and are recommended to all readers. We will not attempt to duplicate the efforts of football historians here. For our purposes a thumb-nail sketch should suffice to set the scene.

The rules of play in existence when The Football Association was founded varied from one school or college to another so that when students moved on to other colleges and universities new rules had to be learned. Also, confusion arose when schools agreed to meet on the football field. Before a match could be played the rules of each school had to be debated and agreement reached as to which set would be adopted. Alternatively, a compromise set of rules was drafted.

By the mid-nineteenth century two distinct patterns of play had emerged. On the one hand, there were colleges which, though differing on various points of local law and tradition, were agreed on the all-important method of kicking and dribbling the ball with the feet. On the other hand several important institutions, likewise separated by local considerations, favoured carrying the ball and permitted the tripping and hacking of opponents.

When The Football Association first met in 1863, to determine a common method of play for all matches organized within its jurisdiction, it was intended that the chosen method would embrace the most desirable features of both the dribbling and the handling codes. The choice was not easy, for feelings ran high amongst the two groups of protagonists. The handful of men who gathered in the gloom of oil lamps in the Freemason's Tavern, Great Queen Street, Lincoln's Inn Fields in London, on a cold grey December day in 1863, may have been aware of the possible consequences of their deliberations, but they could not in their wildest dreams have imagined the extent to which the game of football would intoxicate the world within a century.

The Freemason's Tavern, Great Queen Street, Lincoln's Inn Fields

At this stormy meeting was adopted a set of rules of play based on those in use at Cambridge University. Because these rules excluded 'running with the ball and hacking of opponents' as legal practices, Mr F.W. Campbell withdrew

I.

The maximum **length of the ground** shall be 200 yards, the maximum **breadth** shall be 100 yards, the length and breadth shall be marked off with flags and the **goal** shall be defined by two upright posts, 8 yards apart, without any tap or bar across them.

II.

The Game shall be commenced by a **place kick** from the centre of the ground by the side winning the toss, the other side shall not approach within 10 yards of the ball until it is kicked off. After a goal is won the losing side shall be entitled to kick off.

III.

The two sides shall change goals after each goal is won.

IV.

A goal shall be won when the ball passes over the space between the goal posts (at whatever height), not being thrown, knocked on, or carried.

V.

When the ball is in **touch** the first player who touches it shall kick or throw it from the point on the boundary line where it left the ground, in a direction at right angles with the boundary line.

VI.

A player shall be **out of play** immediately he is in front of the ball, and must return behind the ball as soon as possible. If the ball is kicked past a player by his own side, he shall not touch or kick it or advance until one of the other side has first kicked it or one of his own side on a level with or in front of him has been able to kick it.

VII.

In case the ball goes behind the goal line, if a player on the side to whom the goal belongs first touches the ball, one of his side shall be entitled to a free kick from the goal line at the point opposite the place where the ball shall be touched. If a player of the opposite side first touches the ball, one of his side shall be entitled to a free kick from a point 15 yards outside the goal line, opposite the place where the ball is touched.

VIII.

If a player makes a **fair catch** he shall be entitled to a **free kick**, provided he claims it by making a mark with his heel at once; and in order to take such kick he may go as far back as he pleases, and no player on the opposite side shall advance beyond his mark until he has kicked.

IX.

A player shall be entitled to run with the ball towards his adversaries' goal if he makes a fair catch, or catches the ball on the first bound; but in the case of a fair catch, if he makes his mark, he shall not then run.

X.

If any player shall run with the ball towards his adversaries' goal, any player on the opposite side shall be at liberty to charge, hold, trip, or hack him, or to wrest the ball from him; but no player shall be held and hacked at the same time.

the Blackheath Club from membership of the infant Football Association. Eight years later the Rugby Union was formed and from then on 'football' and 'rugby football' were irrevocably separated.

Ironically, some years later the Blackheath Club, one of the founders of the Rugby Union, led the campaign to ban 'hacking' from the rugby game. 'Hacking' was defined as 'kicking an adversary of the front of the leg below the knee'.

(Left and below) The first printed version of the 1863 laws

XI.

Neither tripping or hacking shall be allowed, and no player shall use his hands or elbows to hold or push his adversary, except in the case provided for by Law X.

XII.

Any player shall be allowed to charge another, provided they are both in active play. A player shall be allowed to charge if even he is out of play.

XIII.

A player shall be allowed to throw the ball or pass it to another if he make a fair catch, or catches the ball on the first bound.

XIV.

No player shall be allowed to wear projecting nails, iron plates, or gutta percha on the soles or heels of his boots.

DEFINITION OF TERMS.

A Place Kick—Is a Kick at the Ball while it is on the ground, in any position which the Kicker may choose to place it.

A Free Kick—Is the privilege of Kicking the Ball, without obstruction, in such manner as the Kicker may think fit.

A Fair Catch—Is when the Ball is Caught, after it has touched the person of an Adversary or has been kicked, knocked on, or thrown by an Adversary, and before it has touched the ground or one of the Side catching it; but if the Ball is kicked from out of touch, or from behind goal line, a fair Catch cannot be made.

Hacking—Is kicking an Adversary on the front of the leg, below the knee.

Tripping—Is throwing an Adversary by the use of the legs without the hands, and without hacking or charging.

Charging—Is attacking an Adversary with the shoulder, chest, or body, without using the hands or legs.

Knocking on—Is when a Player strikes or propels the Ball with his hands, arms or body, without kicking or throwing it.

Holding—Includes the obstruction of a Player by the hand or any part of the arm below the elbow.

Touch—Is that part of the field, on either side of the ground, which is beyond the line of flags.

In fourteen simple rules, now to be known as the Laws of the Game, The Football Association had spelt out the method of play. Since 1863 many changes have been made to the wording of these laws but the basic principles of play have survived – a lasting testimony to the wisdom of the founders of the modern game. Unlike today's version of the laws of the game there was no mention of the 'spirit' in which the game should be played, highlighted some hundred and three years later by the International Board as being 'of paramount importance'.

However, the chosen method of play, and subsequent changes of emphasis introduced by the game's legislators, provide pointers towards the underlying principles of the spirit of the game.

Basic principles

1   EQUALITY

The first principle is that those who take part in the game must have an equal opportunity to demonstrate individual skills. By outlawing certain acts of physical contact such as the tripping, hacking, pushing and holding of opponents, all of which could be put under a general heading of 'unfair play', the game has been transformed from an ancient, rough-and-tumble, violent and dangerous activity into a sport where skill is to be admired and encouraged.

A Heath cartoon of 1830 (the original belongs to Arsenal Football Club)

Physical strength and size are not prerequisites for an individual to be able to show skill. This point is easily demonstrated in the composition of modern football teams. For example, the top eight teams of the 1974 World Cup championships in the Federal Republic of Germany produced the following variations in height and weight amongst individuals considered to be some of the world's most talented and skilful players:

Team	Player	Height (cm)	Weight (kg)
Germany (FR)	Beckenbauer	181	75
Netherlands	Cruyff	180	70
Poland	Tomaszewski	192	93
Brazil	José Guimaraes	169	61
Germany (DR)	Croy	186	80
Sweden	Olsson	168	62
Agentina	Houseman	167	65
Yugoslavia	Dzajic	174	77

The extremes of physical size were represented by the following:

		Height
Poland	Tomaszewski	192 cm
Zaïre	Mana	157 cm

		Weight
Poland	Gorgon	94 kg
Haiti	Léandre	56 kg

Players of small physical size can and do reach the highest level of competitive football. In most cases the speed and powers of manoeuvre of the small players puts them on level terms with opponents of greater power and strength. This is a major reason why the soccer version of football has become so popular in America, where the traditional rugby version puts the player of small physique at a severe disadvantage. Thus, equality of opportunity has been provided for all players to demonstrate individual skills. We shall see later other ways in which legislators have written the equality principle into the laws.

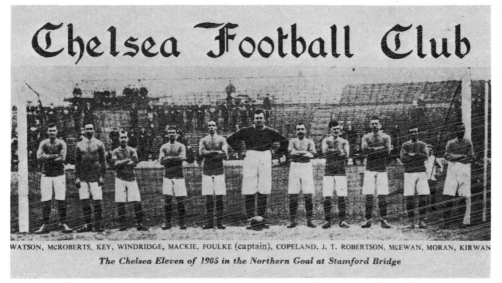

WATSON, MCROBERTS, KEY, WINDRIDGE, MACKIE, FOULKE (captain), COPELAND, J. T. ROBERTSON, MCEWAN, MORAN, KIRWAN

The Chelsea Eleven of 1905 in the Northern Goal at Stamford Bridge

Extremes of physical size are also clear in this photograph of the Chelsea team of 1905

2 SAFETY

The second principle, in contrast with the violence and danger generated in ancient football, is that the health of the players must be safeguarded in normal match play. Great care has been exercised in specifying the components – the size of the playing area and the equipment of the players – so as to reduce hazards and promote a healthy environment without restricting skill too severely. Examples will be given later to underline the observance of the principle of safety in the written law.

3 ENJOYMENT

The third principle is that the game should provide the maximum pleasure for all who take part. To provide a framework within which football can continue to be an enjoyable experience, legislators have identified certain acts of behaviour as unfair, unsporting, or just plain unacceptable. Strict punishments are incorporated to make it unprofitable for those who choose to ignore the basic code of gentlemanly behaviour expected of them. The enjoyment of football owes much to the determination of past and present legislators to preserve this fundamental philosophy.

Equality, safety, enjoyment – three simple words, three vital principles dovetailed into the laws. But how can they be seen at work within the many ordinary words that form the text of the laws?

Law groups

Before searching for the three basic principles it helps to look at the laws thematically rather than taking them in strict order from one to seventeen. Studying the laws in the sequence in which they are published implies that they are all of equal importance. This is not true. The laws fall naturally into the four following groups:

GROUP A - COMPONENTS

The laws in this group specify the components required before any organized football match can be played. Components comprise the following:

Law 1   the field of play
Law 2   the ball
Law 3   the number of players
Law 4   players' equipment

Until these laws have been observed the other thirteen remain inoperative.

GROUP B - AUTHORITY

As the group title implies there are laws which deal with authority within the game. Of particular concern to match officials are:

Law 5   referees
Law 6   linesmen

GROUP C - RULES OF PLAY

There are several laws which are, in effect, the rules of play. These deal with the method of play. The pattern is the same as with many other games, for example basketball, cricket, baseball, hockey, table-tennis and billiards. In these, as in football, after preparing or assembling the components come rules which explain the mechanics of the game, how to start, how to score, when a game is won or lost, and so on. In football the rules are contained as follows:

Law 7	duration of the game
Law 8	the start of play
Law 9	ball in and out of play
Law 10	method of scoring
Law 13	free kick

Note This law does not say why a free kick is awarded. It simply explains the mechanics of putting the ball into play.

Law 14	penalty kick

Note As with Law 13 this does not state the reason for the penalty kick, only the procedure of restarting play.

Law 15	throw-in
Law 16	goal kick
Law 17	corner kick

Note The last three laws deal with the method of restarting play after the ball has crossed a boundary line.

GROUP D - TECHNICAL

The remaining two laws deal with situations which occur when the ball is in play and may be conveniently described as technical laws, namely:

Law 11	off-side
Law 12	fouls and misconduct

Grouping the laws in this manner underlines the function of each law and its relationship with others in the same group. The group titles, which describe the general theme of each group, can easily be remembered by the mnemonic method of putting together the first letters to form a simple word. Thus *components – authority – rules – technical* become CART.

The spirit within the law

To unlock the basic principles of the spirit of the game from the written word, we need to find a key which opens the door to the minds of legislators who, over more than a century, have framed, adjusted, revised, re-phrased and summarized every word of football law whilst ensuring that the fundamental principles remained intact. The key is a simple three-letter word, a word which has probably driven more parents of small children to distraction than any other. The key word is – *why?*

This is how it works. A statement is chosen from a law, the key word is applied and the statement is analysed to discover how the basic principles of the spirit of the game are built into it. By taking several examples, we can see emerging a clear picture of the spirit in operation throughout all seventeen laws.

GROUP A – COMPONENTS (LAWS 1, 2, 3 and 4)

Law 1 – The field of play

The first statement reads 'The field of play shall be rectangular'. WHY? Why should football be played on a *rectangular* field? Can the game be played on a field which is square? Or on a field which is rectangular but with the goal-lines longer than the touchlines? Why should the law insist that 'the length shall in all cases exceed the breadth?' There must be a reason. What are the basic principles which apply in this statement?

The answer lies in analysing a situation within the experience of every football player or official who prepares himself physically before a new season. After completing an arduous training session, probably including sprinting, stamina running, physical exercises and weight-lifting, our enthusiast is nearing the point of exhaustion. But, incredible though it seems, before collapsing into a hot bath or cooling off under a shower, he finds a reserve of energy to join in a practice game of football with his club-mates or colleagues. Quickly, teams of five, six or seven or more a side are decided. A formally marked field is not available, but makeshift goals are established with the aid of tracksuit tops, shoes, bags, and any other object which can serve as a goalpost marker.

As the practice match proceeds there are two situations which invariably arise to spoil the enjoyment of the game for most of those playing. First, the ball is kicked far beyond the goals and valuable time is lost while it is being retrieved. Second, and more boring, is the situation where two opposing players are contesting possession of the ball far out to the sides of the unmarked field. While the two opponents are enjoying an active part in the game the rest of the players are, in effect, excluded from taking part. It is here that tempers become short and the level of enjoyment falls quickly, simply because there is no restriction of play at the sides of the makeshift field. After all, one of the main objects of playing the game is to put the ball into the targets, the goals. All play, to remain interesting and enjoyable, should aim for this simple objective. Any factor designed to encourage the flow of play between the target areas must contribute towards the enjoyment of the game. Thus, by the simple expedient of insisting that the field of play shall always be rectangular, legislators have provided a practical example of the third principle of the spirit of the game – enjoyment.

Figure 1 shows four stages in the evolution of the field of play.

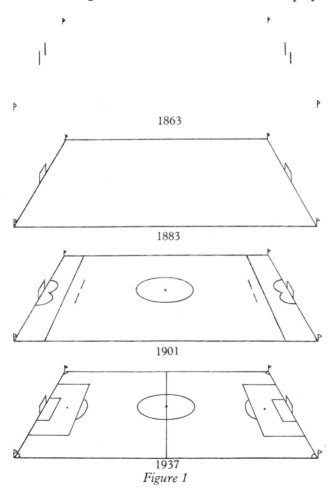

Figure 1

Here are examples of the second principle – safety:

Size of field   When first specified the field was allowed to be a maximum of two hundred yards long by a hundred yards wide. In 1897 it was decided that the playing area was too large. The maximum length was reduced to a hundred and thirty yards. Apart from radically affecting the tactics of play and increasing the enjoyment of goal-area activity, the health of the players was less severely taxed than when they had played on the larger area. Any reader who has taken part in five-a-side games on a full-sized field will have experienced the excessive physical effort required to maintain top performance.

Markings   The brief requirement that lines shall not be marked by a V-shaped rut is clearly intended to safeguard players from injury.

Cornerposts   That they shall be 'not less than five feet (1.5 metres) high and with a non-pointed top' reduces the element of risk to players. Shorter posts would be very dangerous.

By posing the key question *why?* to other parts of Law 1, it is possible to find more examples of the three principles at work. The reader is invited to use this approach to determine which principles apply, for example, in the choice of one yard (one metre) for the corner radius, and how the size of the goals incorporates all three basic principles of equality, safety and enjoyment.

Law 2 – The ball

'The ball shall be spherical.' Why? Can we not play the game with a cube? We can, as any reader who has enjoyed, as a child, kicking a cardboard box will recall. Can we not play the game with a can-shaped ball? Certainly. Again, most readers will have enjoyed football games with cans. Similarly, other shapes can serve as the ball – as illustrated in figure 2.

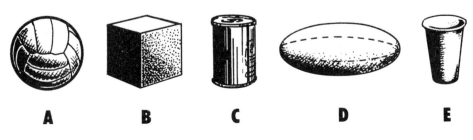

A   **B**   **C**   **D**   **E**

Figure 2

Shape E, a paper cup, may appear to be taking this point too far, but a personal experience in South Africa suggests otherwise. A soccer skills tournament organized by Coca-Cola for schoolboys was in progress at the Orlando Stadium, Soweto, near Johannesburg. Individual boys were required to demonstrate their skills by moving a ball with feet or head around an obstacle course. Time taken and manner of performance were the features on which contestants were judged. The tournament was interesting, but of equal fascination was a 'football match' in progress behind one of the goals, where thirty to forty contestants, who had either completed their test or were waiting to be called, were generating much excitement and pleasure playing with a ball which was a Coca-Cola paper cup. Those boys were not prevented from playing an enjoyable game because Law 2 restricts the shape of the ball. So why should the law insist on one shape? What are the special qualities of a sphere? Which basic principles of the spirit of the game are observed by this requirement?

The answer can be observed in any group of children with a ball: the ball is never still, is constantly on the move from hand to hand, being bounced, thrown or kicked from one to another. In our very young days we learn that a ball is a friendly object, smooth to the touch, with no projections to cause pain; it rolls when pushed and returns if properly treated. In other words we found magic in being able to create dynamic situations with an inanimate object. Could a cube hold the same fascination? No. If it were pushed, it would stop; if dropped, it would not bounce. By comparison it is a lifeless, uninteresting object.

As we grew, we learned to create a great variety of dynamic situations by throwing, kicking and heading, using limbs and trunk to experiment and to achieve a measure of self-expression. Nothing else was required for enjoyment. We did not need a field, goals, other players, rules or referees. We had our own separate little world. Later at school we were provided with opportunities to share pleasures with others in playing organized ball games. The game of Association Football was one of the games in which a spherical ball was used, and we gained new experiences and new enjoyment in taking part in a team, developing, unconsciously, a team spirit, enjoying the pride of performance of our team and comparing our own skills with those of others.

The ball measures and reproduces the skill of the player. It is the only object which provides the player with an equal opportunity to demonstrate his skill – the definition of the first principle of equality. The second principle, safety, is incorporated in the statement that '… no material shall be used in its construction which might prove dangerous to the players'.

Law 4 – Players' equipment

Passing over Law 3 – it is not our intention to comment on all seventeen laws – we find that Law 4 is one of the longest in the law book. The message of safety is clear enough, being summed up neatly in the opening twelve words of the law: '(1) A player shall not wear anything which is dangerous to another player.' And yet the law deals exhaustively, using nearly four hundred words, with things which project from the soles of footwear worn while playing the game. The words describe bars and studs, studs moulded as an integral part of the sole, combined bars and studs, leather, rubber, aluminium, plastic or similar; shapes, sizes, screw-in studs; metal seatings and other technical terms which may appear to be intended to mislead rather than to inform. Why all this fuss about footwear? Can football not be played unless footwear includes projections from the soles? Why should not the law simply end after the opening twelve words? Permitting these projections seems to be contrary to the principle of safety.

One of the great attractions of the game, and a major reason why it has spread around the globe, is that it can be played on practically any surface, from thick mud to concrete. It has been recognized that on certain surfaces players need some help in maintaining balance and agility in order to demonstrate their skills. By permitting footwear projections the first principle of equality is observed; by rigidly controlling this element of danger, the safety principle is applied, and because players are better able to produce their skills, more of the third principle, enjoyment is evident.

GROUP C – RULES OF PLAY (LAWS 7, 8, 9, 10, 13, 14, 15, 16 and 17)

For reasons which will be apparent later, Group B will be the final group to be analysed. In Group C examples of the basic principles in two laws should suffice to give the picture of the spirit at work.

Law 7 – Duration of the game

'The duration of the game shall be two equal periods of forty-five minutes …' is the statement to be questioned. Why two periods? Why not one period of ninety minutes, or three or four of shorter duration? Is the answer simply to change the goals defended by each team so that any inequality in relation to the field of play, direction of wind or sun, or any other influencing factor, may be balanced during the second period? This would certainly satisfy the first principle of equality. It is of interest here to note that the earliest rules appeared to deal with inequalities in direction of play in a more practical manner, by requiring the teams to change ends after a goal was scored. If no goals were scored within half of the allotted playing time then the teams changed ends.

The effect of two equal periods on the enjoyment of the game can be illustrated by means of a graph. In figure 3 the level of enjoyment is measured on the vertical scale against time, the horizontal scale.

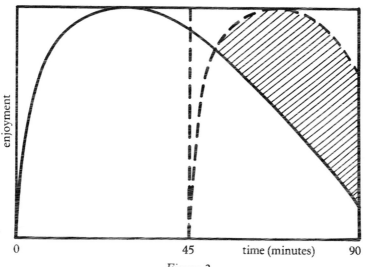

Figure 3

We see that if a game is played non-stop for the full period of ninety minutes the level of enjoyment should rise quickly when the players are fresh. It would then be expected to fall away rapidly as players become tired, lose concentration or patience, and as their level of performance deteriorates. Another childhood experience confirms this theory. Children will play football for hours non-stop until exhaustion overtakes their level of enjoyment.

By cutting the game into two periods and providing the players with a short interval to gather their energies for the second half, we expect that the level of enjoyment will rise quickly to the peak achieved in the first period and that it

C

will be maintained almost constantly until the end of play. The two-period game is shown as a dotted line. The shaded portion is the amount of extra enjoyment achieved compared with the one-period game. A three- or four-period game is unlikely to add to the level of enjoyment. Although players should be better able to cope physically with shorter periods, their extra effort is likely to be countered by time lost in building to peak performance after the second and third breaks, and the final period is likely to be the least enjoyable.

Law 7 is therefore framed to provide:

1   equality in sharing the allotted time in the direction of play
2   safety, by providing an interval to regain strength
3   enjoyment to its theoretical maximum by playing two periods.

Law 13 – Free kick

The first point to be questioned is the title of this law. What is meant by the word 'free'? Does this mean something for nothing? Clearly not, because elsewhere in the laws a free kick is awarded when a player of the offending team has committed an unfair or unsporting act. He has, in effect, disturbed the condition of equality by preventing his opponents from scoring a goal or making a skilful move, or he has endeavoured to gain an unfair advantage. The free kick is the device used to try and regain the balance of equality lost when the offence was committed. The side offended against may have suffered dearly when this occurred and is entitled to some compensation.

The wording of the law places much emphasis on the position of opposing players before the kick is taken. It now becomes clear that the title of the law really means a *free (from obstruction) kick*. This is confirmed by reference to the definition provided by the FA as an addendum to its first laws of the game in 1863: 'A free kick is the privilege of kicking the ball, without obstruction, in such manner as the kicker may think fit.'

An unsatisfactory feature of modern football is the practice of defending players forming a 'wall' between the ball and the goal. In many games it seems that the practice is condoned by the official in charge who delays the kick until the obstructing wall has been formed at the correct distance from the ball. Officials who disregard the pleas of the attacking team to allow the kick to be taken quickly are not aware of, or have forgotten, the true intention of Law 13. Law 13 is about equality – equality of opportunity to demonstrate skill. Its implementation in the practical conduct of play was the subject of a memorandum issued by the FA in 1951. The full text is as follows:

> In order to carry out the spirit of the law relating to free kicks, referees and players are reminded that there must be no undue delay in allowing the non-offending side to take a free kick. This is especially so if the award is a direct free kick. Unnecessary delay often means that inadequate compensation is made for the offence.
>
> Law 13 in no way justifies a referee allowing the side at fault ample opportunity to consolidate its defence: and it certainly does not relieve him from taking action against a player who purposely prevents a free kick from being taken quickly, or who does not at once retire to the proper distance (ten yards from the ball wherever possible). Such a player is committing a further offence and the decision of the council of December 1910 is still applicable: 'Players who do not retire to the proper distance when a free kick is taken must be *cautioned*, and, on any repetition, be *ordered off*. It is particularly requested of referees that attempts to delay the taking of a free kick, by encroaching, should be treated as serious misconduct.'

The FA council Decision of 1910 is now incorporated as Decision 2 of the International Board applicable to Law 13. Note that referees are instructed that they *must* caution players who offend against this decision – no doubt here about the intention of the law administrators. Note also the final two words of the decision: not just plain misconduct, which is bad enough, but *serious misconduct*. The message could not be clearer on the duty of the referee to safeguard the basic principle of equality in this law.

GROUP D – TECHNICAL (LAWS 11 and 12)

Law 11 – Off-side

Why off-side? Can football not be played without the off-side law? As children we were not prevented from playing the game. We ignored off-side and enjoyed ourselves. So what is the point of this law which causes more controversy than the rest of the laws put together?

Thousands of words have been published explaining the situations where a player is considered to be 'off-side', 'out of play', 'off the strength' (in military terms), but too few which explain *why* a player should be penalized for putting himself in these positions. Again, we can relate to childhood games of football. Who was the boy we hated most? The 'goal-hanger', the 'poacher', or some other uncomplimentary term for the boy who placed himself close to the opposing goalkeeper in order to score the goals. Why did we hate this boy so much? It was not that he was contravening Law 11 of the laws of the game. We knew nothing of the requirements of such a formal rule. And yet something within us said that what he was doing was not right. He was doing the least work, seeking the glory of scoring the goals, and not attempting to put any real skill into the play. In terms of basic principles we recognized even at the age of six or seven that football was more enjoyable if all players made an attempt to demonstrate their skills. We despised the lazy player, the player who sought the glory without providing the effort.

The rules of the Eton College game of football of 1862 exposed the inner feelings of legislators by stating in the off-side law: 'A player is considered to be "sneaking" when only three, or less than three, of the opposite side, are before him, and the ball behind him, and in such cases he may not kick the ball'. The dictionary definition of a sneak is 'a mean, servile fellow: a petty thief'. The reason for Law 11 now becomes more understandable because it is aimed at such despicable people. The restriction on players who do not comply with the first principle of demonstrating skill helps towards the observance of the third principle of gaining the maximum enjoyment from the game.

Law 12 – Fouls and misconduct

In the next chapter the practical nature of fouls and misconduct is discussed at some length. Here we shall determine how Law 12 fits the philosophy of the game. It is bordering of the facetious to ask – why Law 12? Can we play football without it? And yet the game was played for centuries without it. But not the game we know today. The fundamental difference between ancient and modern football is skill. Skill could not survive the hurly burly, mass of bodies, the violence and confusion of the old-time game.

In the opening paragraph of Law 12 physical contact is severely restricted by defining certain actions, which, if committed intentionally, are not to be tolerated. This does not mean that all forms of physical contact are forbidden. In every match players are kicked, pushed, struck or held without any sanction being necessary because it happens accidentally and in the run of the game, and it is accepted as part and parcel of a healthy physical sport. The important qualification, the one offence which is outlawed in this first section of the law, is *intention*. A player must not obliterate the skill of opponents by intentionally committing (or, in certain cases, even attempting to commit) any of the listed offences. The first principle is clearly in operation here.

Why should handling the ball be considered as serious as kicking, striking or pushing an opponent? Because it offends against the chosen method of play, the first major decision that separated the dribbling and the handling codes of play.

In the middle section of the law, dealing with less serious but still unacceptable practices, the principle of safety is clearly seen in the punishment of players who 'play in a manner considered by the referee to be dangerous, e.g. attempting to kick the ball while held by the goalkeeper'. The player is not intentionally directing an assault on the goalkeeper's person, but he must consider the danger involved to his opponent and moderate his challenge accordingly.

Enjoyment is at the root of the whole of Law 12, for no player will enjoy being on the receiving end of any of the illegal physical acts; the game will be less enjoyable for all if obstruction is not controlled or if goalkeepers are allowed excessive possession of the ball or indulge in delaying tactics. In the last section, the code of personal conduct, which should provide a healthy and enjoyable environment for all involved, is implied by reference to acts which are unacceptable. These are discussed in more detail later.

GROUP B - AUTHORITY (LAWS 5 and 6)

This group has been placed last because, in theory, the two laws are unnecessary.

Law 5 - Referees

Why Law 5? Is it necessary, in order to play football, to add a referee to the twenty-two players? It was not considered necessary when the FA adopted its first set of laws. Football was a game played in a gentlemanly fashion - that is, in the disciplinary environment of schools and colleges or by the Old Boys' clubs of football-playing establishments. Differences of opinion were settled in a sporting manner between the two captains, although it is recorded that sometimes blows were struck in the process. Some institutions required umpires to be appointed by the teams. Each umpire was stationed in the half of the field defended by his own team. Only when an appeal was made by a player was an umpire required to make a decision. Later if one could not decide the right course of action, the umpires conferred. Then a referee appeared on the scene, stationed at the halfway line outside the field of play. When the umpires could not agree the problem was taken to the referee.

Competitive football in the form of the FA Challenge Cup in 1871, the formation of the Football League in 1888, and the growth of professional football, all increased the number of disputes in matches. Play was interrupted more frequently while disputes were settled. In order to guide match officials the FA issued the following memorandum in 1886:

> Rule 13:   In the event of an appeal for any supposed infringement of the Laws, the ball shall be in play until a decision has been given.
>
> Umpires should remember how very important it is, for the proper working of this Law, that their decisions should be given as quickly as possible. If a claim is made and one Umpire allows it, the Referee, if he agrees with him, should instantly sound his whistle, without waiting to ascertain the opinion of the other Umpire; it being of course understood that the system which has been found to work so well in the past is to be continued in the future, viz., that the Umpires should allow an appeal by holding up a stick, and the Referee by sounding his whistle.

Five years later the problems became so acute that the referee went into the middle and the umpires went to the touchline – the beginnings of the diagonal system in use today.

The competitive element had driven the legislators to employ a neutral official to enforce the laws and decide disputed points. It is of interest to record that it was not until 1973 that the duty of the referee to decide disputed points was taken out of Law 5. So the referee had become essential in maintaining the principle of enjoyment in football. Over the years he has been given greater authority and responsibility. It has never been more vital than it is today for match officials to be fully aware of their role in the game.

The safety of players is a major consideration for referees. Law 5 requires play to be stopped if, in the referee's opinion, a player is seriously hurt. In this context the most important aspect of the law is the so-called 'advantage clause' when the referee is required to '… refrain from penalizing in cases where he is satisfied that by doing so he would be giving an advantage to the offending team.' A common misconception about this clause, even among officials, is that, if a player is tripped, but is able to continue with the ball, play should be allowed to continue so that *he is given an advantage*. But it is not a matter of giving an advantage to the player offended against because, if he had not been tripped, he would in any case have retained possession of the ball. In fact the offending team have been *denied* the advantage they would have gained if play

Figure 4　The Referee: usual dress and equipment

PENCIL
NOTEBOOK

WHISTLE
ATTACHED
TO WRIST

IN POCKET:
COIN
STOPWATCH
EXTRA WHISTLE
EXTRA PENCIL
WRIST WATCH

had been stopped. The application of advantage allows the referee to disregard the written requirements of Law 12. In effect the referee is being allowed *to apply his interpretation of the spirit of the game.*

Another aspect of setting aside the written law in the interests of the game is stated in International Board Decision 8, after Law 5:

> The laws of the game are intended to provide that games should be played with as little interference as possible, and in this view it is the duty of referees to penalize only deliberate breaches of the law.
>
> Constant whistling for trifling and doubtful breaches produces bad feeling and loss of temper on the part of the players and spoils the pleasure of spectators.

An example of a trifling breach would be a player lifting one foot one inch from the ground when taking a throw-in. To stop play and award a throw-in to the opposing side would be correct in the strict application of the written law but against the intention of the laws to provide an enjoyable game of football.

Summary

The governing world authority of football, the International Board, has endeavoured to keep the game as simple as possible by resisting constant attempts to introduce changes to the rules of play. Through successive generations of dedicated administrators it has urged those who take part in the sport to promote and safeguard the principles of true sportsmanship in the name of the spirit of the game. This chapter has tried to establish the substance of the spirit. It is a guide for present and future generations of those who have chosen, as their role in the game, the control of match play. By the use of the analytical method suggested here, a new dimension can be added to the study of the written law – a dimension which should enable the reader of the laws to discover hidden wisdom in the written word.

In the course of a referee's career situations will occur which have not been provided for in written form. He will have to weigh up the problem and resolve it quite simply by asking himself, 'What is the fair solution?' or 'What is the answer in terms of the spirit of the game?'. The quality of his decision will be determined by his comprehension of the spirit of the game. This latter point is nicely summed up in *The Book of Football* (1906): 'We have referees who are temperamentally unable to disregard the printed word – others (all too few) who read between the lines and recognize that the first object should be to ensure the game being played honestly, fairly and in a truly sporting spirit'. It is often said, 'When in doubt, apply Law 18 – common sense.' Perhaps this would be better put, 'When in doubt, apply Law 0 – the spirit of the game'.

3 Football Crime and Punishment

Football and emotion are inseparable. Every individual is an experienced observer of the unbreakable relationship between emotion and conduct in everyday life. It is generally agreed that, to make life bearable, we must accept the disciplines imposed on our conduct by civil laws. Just as civil laws provide a code for living, sports laws provide a code for playing. In our chosen sport, as in many others, the match official's role is concerned with the proper conduct of those who take part. As we saw in the previous chapter, the first object should be to see that the game is played honestly, fairly, and in a truly sporting spirit.

In order to safeguard the ideals of the sport it is not sufficient that the match official be totally aware of its basic philosophy. Just as the policeman has to be totally aware of offences against public welfare so the match official has to be totally aware of the crimes, the violations, of football law which bring these ideals into disrepute. He must also be aware of the punishment prescribed for varying degrees of crime and the power which is put into his hands to match the punishment with the crime. This chapter discusses the physical acts and the type of conduct which are considered illegal in football and some guidance is given, through illustration, towards accurate recognition of football crime.

But what is football crime? Analysing football law it seems that crimes can be classified generally as (1) physical crimes -- committed against other persons, and 2) crimes of misconduct, or offences against the spirit of the game. From Law 12, offences can be gathered under these two headings as follows:

1 Crimes against the person

a) fouls
b) dangerous play
c) charging at the wrong time
d) obstruction
e) charging the goalkeeper
f) serious foul play
g) violent conduct

2   Crimes of misconduct

a) illegalities
b) persistent infringements
c) dissent

d) ungentlemanly conduct
e) insulting language
f) persistent misconduct

1   Crimes against the person

Examples of the more obvious types of physical crimes are illustrated in figures 5 to 11.

Figure 5   Kicking an opponent

Figure 6   Tripping an opponent

Figure 7   Jumping at an opponent

Figure 8   Charging violently or dangerously

Figure 9   Striking an opponent

Figure 10   Holding an opponent

Figure 11   Pushing an opponent

a) *Fouls*

Eight types of fouls are described, all committed as physical acts against an opponent. The law is specific in stating that these acts are illegal only if committed *with intention*, with a purpose to hurt, or to prevent the opponent from carrying out an act of skilful play. In short - unfair play.

How does the referee recognize intent? It would be unfair for a player who makes or attempts to make physical contact to be punished under this section of the law if, in fact, he did not intend to kick, trip, jump at, charge in a violent or dangerous manner, or to commit any of the remaining five offences. To be one hundred per cent correct the referee would need to be inside the mind of the player at the instant he decided to do whatever it was which caused him to come under suspicion of breaking the law. Because this is impossible it follows that the referee will sometimes be wrong and, quite naturally, the player incorrectly found guilty will react in some manner which could contravene another part of Law 12 and lead to further punishment. Who is at fault, the player or the referee? It is unsatisfactory in this situation to accuse the player of lack of control, of unsportsmanlike behaviour, even though at times this may be a valid accusation. Who made the faulty judgement? Not the player.

The point of dwelling on the subject of intent is to stress the fact to the referee that his major task in making correct calls under this section of Law 12 is to work to reduce his rate of error! A young and raw recruit who has had little experience of life, of judging the emotions and actions of others, is certain to show a higher percentage of error in his assessments of intent than a more mature, experienced, official. How can the new recruit be helped to rapidly reduce his error percentage and the experienced official to improve on his? In chapter 8, where the subject of reading a game is discussed, a method of approach is suggested.

b) *Dangerous play*

Looking at the offence of dangerous play we have a slightly easier task. All that is required is for the referee to decide whether or not an *unintentional* act of physical contact, or attempted contact, could be considered as dangerous to the opponent. The classic example of an attacker attempting to kick the ball while it is held by the goalkeeper is illustrated in figure 12. There should be no doubt about the danger here and action must be taken by the official in charge. At the same time it must be made clear that all unintentional physical contact is not to be considered dangerous. For example fair charging when the ball is within playing distance is a legitimate action intended to catch the opponent off balance and gain possession of the ball (see figure 13). No player has the right to uncontested possession.

Figure 12   *Figure 13*

Where the referee draws the line is entirely a matter of his personal opinion at the instant of observing the action. He can never be wrong in the context of the law because it is *his* opinion which constitutes the judgement of dangerous play. However, what is important is that the individual official should become aware of what is and what is not generally acceptable in physical play. It is pertinent at this point to refer back to the previous chapter, to Decision 8 relevant to Law 5, viz., 'constant whistling for trifling and doubtful breaches produces bad feeling and loss of temper on the part of the players and spoils the pleasure of spectators'.

c)   *Charging at the wrong time*

In Law 12 it is an offence to charge fairly, that is, with the shoulder, at the wrong time, when the ball is not within playing distance and the two players concerned are definitely not trying to play it. What is the charging player trying to do? Either to get a better chance to play the ball the way he chooses, when it arrives, or to prevent the opponent from making contact or from moving into a more advantageous position.

What is 'playing distance'? – a question which frequently causes much discussion among officials because it is vague. Some would prefer an exact distance to be specified to reduce differences in interpretation amongst officials. One rough guide provided by the FA in its Memorandum on Refereeing No. 5 of 1951 is two to three yards.

It is inadvisable to be more specific because the ball can be moving towards or away from the players; at right angles or parallel to the direction in which they are facing; up or down; fast or slow; or in any combination of these. Officials who have played the game (probably ninety-nine per cent of all referees) will have practical experience of when a ball is considered to be within playing distance.

d)   *Obstruction*

As will be seen in the next chapter, where obstruction is discussed in detail, 'playing distance' was further defined by the FIFA Referees' Committee in 1969. Figures 14 and 15 illustrate the unfair obstruction of an opponent.

Figure 14   Obstruction is penalised when a player blocks the opponent's path to the ball when it is not within playing distance

Figure 15   Obstruction by running between an opponent and the ball

The obstruction clause was not intended to penalize every situation where the player appeared between ball and opponent because, in the run of play, this will occur many times naturally and fairly. As with fouls, the referee has to judge the *intention* of the interposing player. A player who is shielding the ball from an opponent with his body and is not touching the ball is not obstructing, provided that he can play the ball if he so wishes (Decision 7, see figure 16). In this situation he is not permitted to move back into his opponent, that is, away from the ball, in order to prevent the opponent from challenging for the ball. This action becomes the more serious offence of pushing an opponent with the body.

Figure 16 An example of 'screening' the ball from an opponent, which is not obstruction because the ball is being played

e) Charging the goalkeeper

The goalkeeper *may* be charged fairly if he is holding the ball, is obstructing an opponent or has passed outside his goal area. He *may not* be charged inside his own goal area when not holding the ball. Why should the goalkeeper be allowed the privilege of an unmolested challenge for the ball inside his own area? The answer lies in the practice which developed in the 1890s of goalkeepers being allowed the privilege of using their hands to control or gain possession of the ball. Opposing forwards thought this was too much and made the goalkeeper the target of violent charges, whether he was in possession or not. Consequently, serious injuries were sustained by goalkeepers and more protection was written into the law, but only within the area of the goal.

f) Serious foul play

The law requires the referee to send off the field of play any player who is, in his opinion, guilty of serious foul play. What is *serious* foul play? Surely, *all* foul play is serious. Why the distinction? It is a matter of degree and means; to put it simply, if any of the eight fouls are committed *in a serious manner*, a more severe punishment will be applied. Again, we rely on the understanding of the spirit of the game in the mind and heart of the referee to make the correct distinction, for there is no clear dividing line between an 'ordinary' foul and a 'serious' foul.

Figure 17   Serious foul play

A valid definition of serious foul play would be a physical act of excessive force or violence committed with the premeditated intention of harming an opponent or preventing him from completing a skilful move. A crime sheet of offences within this definition would include:

    i)   kicking or striking an opponent when the ball is out of play

    ii)   butting an opponent with the head

    iii)   stamping on an opponent who has fallen

    iv)   violent pushing or charging when the ball is not within playing distance

    v)   bringing an opponent to the ground with a rugby-type tackle to prevent a goal (figure 17).

    vi)   deliberate tripping or kicking when an opponent is in a good position to score and the offender has no chance to play the ball fairly

    vii)   an 'over-the-top tackle, that is, the sole of the offender's boot is thrust violently at the leg of an opponent, over the top of the ball, and scraped down the shin bone (figure 18)

    viii)   pulling the hair of an opponent

Figure 18 '*Over-the-top' tackle*

g) *Violent conduct*

What is the difference between violent conduct and serious foul play? Serious foul play relates to the specified fouls listed in paragraphs (a) to (h) of Law 12. Violent conduct relates to violent acts directed at persons other than opponents, such as a match official, colleague or spectator. A player who spits at an opponent, an official, or any other person is considered to have acted in a violent manner (Decision 13, Law 12). Other unspecified acts which are totally against the spirit of the game and demand the ultimate punishment of dismissal are behaviour of an obscene nature, indecent exposure, and unmistakeable gestures intended to insult or to ridicule. No player who commits any of these acts of violence against the person or against morality should be allowed to remain on the field of play. The game is better without such players.

2 Crimes of misconduct

With the exception of a few offences which can be described as technical, that is against the rules of play, the nature of crimes of misconduct is not clearly defined. However, by studying Law 12 paragraphs (j) to (p) which give general headings of what is unacceptable, we can, by inversion, determine the code of personal conduct expected from players.

It reads as follows:

1 Understand and observe the laws of the game.
2 Accept the decisions of officials without dissent.
3 Play the game fairly and honestly.
4 Respect your opponents and officials.
5 Exercise discipline in controlling your temper and tongue.

D

In the history of football it has never been possible to achieve total observance of this pure code of ethics. Players are human beings and few human beings are perfect. However, it must always be the unsworn oath of legislators, administrators and match officials to safeguard by personal example the ideals of sportsmanship and fair play and to resist attempts to undermine bedrock principles by those less courageous individuals who would wish to obtain concessions which would ultimately destroy the game. Some of the crimes of misconduct identifiable within the laws or which are observed in practice are as follows:

a)   *Illegalities*

A general heading which covers technical infringements or the non-observance of the playing laws, for example, playing the ball twice at a free kick; incorrect throwing-in procedure, handling the ball (figure 19); illegal entry to or exit from the field of play, excessive possession by goal-keepers.

Figure 19

b)   *Persistent infringments*

The crime of persistent infringement is committed by the player who persistently refuses to observe the laws. But what is meant by persistent? How many times does a player have to break the laws before action is taken against him?

In an important cup tie between professional teams a player was cautioned for committing just two fouls. The first was a dangerous charge on a goalkeeper with an elbow thrust into his neck. The referee awarded a free kick after warning the offender to exercise more care in his challenges. Within minutes the same player committed the same offence and was, quite justifiably in the context of this particular match, cautioned.

This was an unusual situation. It should not be assumed that two offences automatically constitute persistent infringement. The nature of the offences must be taken into account and the manner in which the offender reacts to the first punishment. Some players will make it apparent, by committing a series of minor infringements, that they are not prepared to observe the laws. In most cases all that is necessary to curb this misconduct is to warn the culprit that persistence in his action will bring more severe punishment than the award of free kicks. A few will ignore the advice given and it becomes necessary to implement the prescribed punishment.

c) *Dissent*

The acceptance of the decision of an arbiter is a basic principle of the ethics of sportsmanship. However unpopular the decision and its consequences, however wrong it was seen to be, the decision must be accepted as final. To disagree by word or by action is a crime against the spirit of the game. Outward signs of disagreement vary from a disbelieving shake of the head to voluble gesticulating protest. It is unreasonable to expect players to react like wooden images to an (in their opinion) doubtful off-side decision which nullifies a goal at a vital stage of the game. Nevertheless, in the emotional atmosphere of that particular moment, control must be exercised within reasonable bounds. Displays of temper, petulance, anger or resentment which go beyond these bounds must be actioned.

In military circles a soldier can be charged for the crime of 'dumb insolence', that is, for displaying a contemptuous manner. He shows dissent simply by expression, without speaking or moving. In certain circumstances a referee may be forced to discipline a similar attitude demonstrated by a dissenting player – not necessarily by the issue of a caution; a word or two may suffice. Figure 20 shows a player dissenting from a referee's decision.

Figure 20

d)   *Ungentlemanly conduct*

'Conduct unbecoming of a gentleman' may seem a somewhat old-fashioned crime in the context of sport, but as we have seen certain ethics must be applied if football is to remain a healthy and pleasurable activity. A more acceptable modern term might be 'unsporting conduct'. Whatever it is called the crime is the same. Wisely, legislators have resisted the temptation to issue a grand list of acts considered ungentlemanly. There are too many to list. New forms of ungentlemanly conduct appear every year, so the list would never be up-to-date. It is enough to rely on the discretion of the referee as to what constitutes ungentlemanly conduct. Certain acts which occur more frequently than others can be identified within the laws to guide match officials. Some of these are illustrated in figures 21, 22 and 23.

Figure 21   Ungentlemanly conduct at a free kick: kicking the ball away from the correct position

Figure 22   Distracting, or attempting to distract, an opponent by shouting

Figure 23 Ungentlemanly conduct: pushing when the ball is out of play

e) *Insulting language*

Listed in Law 12 (o) as foul or abusive language, it is clear from what has already been stated that the use of insulting language must be unacceptable and considered a crime against the spirit of the game. There are many forms of insulting language, some using universally understood expressions, others of a more national or even local texture. There is no world textbook of foul or abusive language to which to refer. No doubt, as with forms of ungentlemanly conduct, new words to express insult continue to appear. Apart from speech forms of a specific national or racial origin, language is peculiar to the individual. Sometimes a person who has difficulty in expressing himself will use an expletive to add emphasis. This is not insulting language. A player who uses expletives to criticize himself, for example, when he makes a mistake in passing or controlling the ball, should not be accused of football crime and dismissed from the game. This is a natural reaction, not intended for the ears of others. If it should happen that his expletives reach the ears of the referee a quick word to keep his voice down is enough.

It is the deliberate delivery of words of insult, foul or abusive, towards others which is the crime. The words 'bloody' and 'bastard', while innocuous enough in certain contexts, can become vicious verbal missiles in a highly charged emotional situation on the field of play, provoking an escalating exchange of insults and often leading to violence. In some situations the words need not be addressed directly to the intended target to be actionable. A player may think he is immune from action if he calls to a colleague, 'We've got a stupid bastard of a referee here'. When he is on his way from the field of play, having been dismissed, he will realize his error.

Abusive language is not always easy to identify, particularly if it has a racial implication. Referees who control teams of mixed races or religious groups will need to be especially aware of expressions intended to insult.

f)   *Persistent misconduct*

Players who, as Law 12 (p) states, persist in misconduct after having received a caution must suffer dismissal from play. The word 'persistent' has already been discussed in (b). In the context of law 12 (p) it is not necessary for the referee to wait for the cautioned player to commit the offence for which he was cautioned before sending him from the field. He has only to be convinced that the player continues to ignore the fact that he is required to observe the laws of the game.

The sequel to the incident described in (b) of the player who was cautioned after only two offences was that he was dismissed later in the match for committing another offence. There was no doubt in the mind of the referee that the player appeared to consider that the laws did not apply to him. The decision to dismiss was very unpopular because the player was a favourite of the home team fans, and, as the referee discovered after the game, it happened to be his benefit match! Not unexpectedly, the incident caused much comment. At the same time the referee was convinced that he had meted out justice and was disturbed by the attitude of some administrators and colleagues who thought that he had been over-zealous. From further enquiries the referee learned that the player concerned had become well known for his terrorizing tactics on goalkeepers. His personality was such that home fans applauded him and local referees who were familiar with the situation had apparently allowed him too much licence. Whenever the player's name was mentioned in local refereeing circles, the reaction was usually a wry smile and a wink followed by the observation, 'He gets away with murder!' It then became understandable that the player had developed a distorted view of the applicability of the laws to his own play. How many matches had been unfairly influenced by the excesses of this player? No one will ever know, but it is valid to pose the question - was the fault entirely his?

Summary

From the foregoing comments and the illustrations the reader should be well acquainted with the general nature of football crime. To enable the referee to carry out the first duty required of him in law 5 (a) - to enforce the laws - it is necessary to become efficient at identifying offences against the laws and spirit of the game. This done, the next question is – what does the referee do now? Some form of punishment must be inflicted on the offending player. What is the armoury of punishments available to the referee?

Punishments

Most laws and many International Board decisions prescribe punishments. There are four degrees of punishment:

1 indirect free kick	awarded for minor or technical offences
2 direct free kick	awarded for more serious offences
3 caution	issued as a warning against further infringement or misconduct
4 dismissal	the ultimate punishment which can be inflicted during a match

In certain situations double punishment is inflicted, for example, a caution plus an indirect or direct free kick.

The penalty kick has not been listed as a punishment because it is a special form of direct free kick and is awarded in special circumstances, that is, when a direct free kick offence has been committed by a defending player within his own team's penalty area. It is important that a penalty kick should not be considered as a separate punishment. The questions to be answered by the referee at the instant of an infringement are:

1   What was the offence?

2   Is the correct punishment an indirect or a direct free kick?

3   If the kick is direct was the offender within his own penalty area?

If the answer to 3 is Yes, there is a special procedure to be observed in relation to placing the ball and other points as specified in Law 14.

To define the penalty kick as a separate punishment, accepting the fact that a goal often results from this special kick, is to encourage a weak official to change the order of the questions and sometimes adopt the wrong procedure. The questions then become:

1   Was the offender in his own penalty area?

2   If so, was the offence serious enough for a penalty kick, or would an indirect free kick be adequate punishment?

Matching the punishment to the crime

> My object, all sublime,
> I shall achieve in time,
> Is to let the punishment fit the crime
> The punishment fit the crime.
>   (from Gilbert and Sullivan's *Mikado*)

An apt quotation for the administrator of justice in football.

Having discussed the crimes and noted the punishments which may be inflicted, how can the referee match the punishment to the crime? Is it enough to list the offences described in the laws with the appropriate punishment? It is a start, but not enough to avoid wide differences of interpretation which can only serve to confuse the players. To reduce these differences to a minimum referee coaches concentrate on feeding many incidents to their students, thus ensuring that they are aware of the correct punishments. In many cases a match incident is described by the spoken or written word. When this is the only available method of giving the information, the incident often does not register clearly in the mind of the student. The spoken or written word is often inadequate to capture a frozen instant of a fast-moving game in such a way that the speaker or writer can transmit the mental picture to the student. A solution to this problem is the use of skilfully illustrated match incidents which can demonstrate a technical point of football within the context of a given match. Both coach and student are then studying the same incident.

To simplify the task of matching punishment to crime the spoken or written answer can be eliminated by a visual aid expressed as an X rating of each punishment, thus:

Indirect	X
Direct	XX
Caution	XXX
Dismissal	XXXX

The system illustrated in figure 24 provides a method of impressing on the mind of the referee an instant relationship between offence and award.

Figure 24

Some referees appear to award a different punishment for the same crime depending on where it is committed and by whom. For example, a pushing offence outside the penalty area is correctly punished by a direct free kick, but the same offence committed inside the penalty area by a defender appears to be interpreted as obstruction because the award given is an indirect free kick. Such officials have either failed to recognize the crime and its matching punishment or have failed to demonstrate the basic courage and integrity required of match officials in enforcing the laws. The illustrated match incident system will help to solve the former problem. It will not solve the latter.

The referee's power to punish

A referee should never be in doubt as to the power he has to punish the crimes of football. Law 5 provides enough authority, as the following extracts testify:

> His power of penalizing shall extend to offences committed when play has been temporarily suspended, or when the ball is out of play.
> [He shall:]
> (d)   have discretionary power to stop the game for any infringement of the Laws and to suspend or terminate the game whenever, by reason of the elements, interference by spectators, or other cause, he deems such stoppage necessary.
> (e)   from the time he enters the field of play caution any player guilty of misconduct or ungentlemanly behaviour and, if he persists, suspend him from further participation in the game.
> (f)   allow no person, other than the players and linesmen, to enter the field of play without his permission.
> (g)   send off the field of play any player who, in his opinion, is guilty of violent conduct, serious foul play, or the use of foul or abusive language.

The International Board has extended the referee's authority by requiring him to report acts of misconduct by anyone connected with a match regardless of whether they occur on the field or in its vicinity and at any time before, during, or after the match in question (Decision 4).

An important but seldom appreciated power added in Decision 12 is that the referee may not allow coaching from the boundary lines. It is understandable that he must have authority to deal with foul play and misconduct but how does coaching from the boundary lines affect the spirit of the law? Is it not constructive to allow experienced coaches to guide their teams and individual players during the course of the game? Would not better team play result from a relaxation of this restriction (figure 25)?

Figure 25   Interference by club officials in issuing instructions to players during the game

The answer lies in the first paragraph of Law 3 which states, 'A match shall be played by two teams each consisting of not more than eleven players ...' No mention of a coach here.

The principle of equality is also affected. Were there to be no restriction on coaching, players would not be demonstrating their own skills but those of the coach whose verbal orders could cause confusion, frustration and even loss of temper. Anyone who has played as a child in an organized team, watched by an over-enthusiastic father or teacher, will have experienced these emotions. It is recorded that a match between teams of eleven-year-old boys had to be abandoned by the referee because of persistent verbal intervention by a coaching father.

Taking this to its logical conclusion, a club with sufficient resources could employ enough coaches to surround the field to cover all parts of the team – defence, attack, goalkeeper and so on. This may not be as absurd as it seems when one observes the lengths to which some wealthy clubs will go to gain a fractional advantage over opponents. The coach's proper role in the game is to exercise his skills with players before the match and to analyse play for future instruction. One of the attractions of football is the unexpected. Rigid formations or robot players, marshalled by coaches armed with portable loudspeakers, would surely put a dead hand on a vital pleasure of the game.

Summary

The laws of the game provide an indication of crimes under general headings. These are capable of wide interpretation depending on each official's attitude to the game. It is the constant aim of the International Board to achieve world uniformity of interpretation of the laws, but the means of achieving this desirable aim present a constant educational problem.

By discussion and illustration this chapter has attempted to narrow differences of interpretation so that a sound basis can be adopted by referees for accurate recognition of the more common types of football crimes. Uniformity of interpretation is further discussed in the next chapter. It is one thing to recognize the crime. It is another to determine the correct punishment. Fortunately the degrees of punishment are few, and a method of matching the appropriate action to specific crimes by illustration has been suggested as an aid to those who devote much leisure time to the coaching of new referees.

It is a pleasure to record here a tribute to the service which the referee coach renders to the game and to express the hope that this book will prove of some value to him, too.

*"Of course it was dangerous
kicking — look where
my knee-cap is now"*

4 Uniform Law Interpretation

Realistically, the achievement of one hundred per cent uniformity of interpretation is impossible because so many decisions are based on personal opinion. Two experienced referees watching the same incident can arrive at quite different conclusions as to the intention behind physical contact.

In the coaching of referees it is easy to demonstrate an obviously intentional act in contrast to one which is obviously unintentional. Between those two extremes the edges can become blurred. As the differences narrow so the opinions diverge. We have already mentioned that referees need to work at reducing error percentage in assessing actual intention. The player *knows* what he intended when his outstretched leg caused an opponent to fall, but to form his opinion the referee can only read the clues inherent in the action. If the player has managed to disguise his action so that the clues are obscure, the verdict may go in his favour.

Chapter 8 suggests what the referee can do to improve his reading of players' intentions. In the first section of this chapter official guidelines to the interpretation of fairly common features of play are quoted. In the second section, three subjects are discussed in more detail. They are a) obstruction, b) advantage and c) off-side. Collectively, they represent a sizeable proportion of the referee's problems of interpretation in practical match play.

1   Official guidelines to interpretation

Charging is covered by an FA memorandum:

A charge signifies intention to shoulder an opponent and should not be confused with accidental contact (figure 13). A player is not allowed to charge an opponent in order to let the ball run on to another player of his own side or out of play. In neither case is he attempting to play the ball. A defender, therefore, is not allowed to deliver a fair charge on an attacker who is trying to charge a goalkeeper in possession of the ball, because the defender is not making any attempt to get the ball.

(FA Memorandum 4, November 1949)

Other guidelines are contained in the following memorandum, approved by the FIFA Referees' Committee, and circulated by the FA in 1969:

The Laws of the Game

1   *Dangerous play* Football is a game where body contact occurs and the laws are framed so that the players can play without danger to themselves if their opponents respect both the letter and spirit of the laws. In some countries in membership with FIFA, certain acts are considered automatically by both players and referees to be dangerous and penalized *whether they are dangerous or not*. Each incident must be judged by the referee as it happens and the question of danger rests entirely on his opinion. Such actions must be penalized regardless of the intention of the player.

The following are some examples where countries differ in their interpretation of what is dangerous play:

1.1 *Tackling with the foot lifted from the ground* This may be dangerous, but is not *necessarily* so. The sole of the foot is an effective way of controlling the ball but a player who lifts his foot should be penalized if the referee sees danger to the opponent in the manner in which it is done. If the player intentionally plays over the ball and makes contact with the opponent's leg, this is a serious foul.

1.2 *Tackling with two feet together* The ball acts as a natural 'cushion' between the players. If the two-footed tackle is controlled and made from a short distance away, there is no danger to the opponent. If it is an uncontrolled jump at the ball from a distance, the tackle has certainly a large element of danger to the opponent.

1.3 *Tackling by sliding* This is done by one or both legs outstretched and the same considerations as for the two-footed tackle apply. The player tackling in this way knows that if he misses the ball he may bring his opponent down, in which case he should be penalized for tripping and not dangerous play.

1.4 *Tackling from behind* If the tackle is made for the ball there can be no offence of tripping, but it may be considered as dangerous play.

1.5 *The 'Scissors' kick* This is a clear example of the importance of judging an action according to the situation in which it is performed. A player who kicks or attempts to kick the ball in this way with no other player near him cannot be penalized for dangerous play. The same action with a player nearby would be very dangerous.

1.6 *Dangerous play against goalkeepers* Whilst kicking or attempting to kick the ball whilst in the goalkeeper's possession is universally considered to be dangerous, raising the foot to block the ball as he kicks it from his hands is equally dangerous though it is not always penalized. Attempts to kick the ball powerfully as it is about to come into the goalkeeper's possession are also a common source of danger to goalkeepers (see figure 12).

2   *Jumping at an opponent* A player sometimes jumps at his opponent as if to head the ball in order to prevent his opponent heading it. This player is guilty of the offence of jumping at an opponent (figure 7).

3   *Use of arm* The use of the arm by players to hold off an opponent is increasing. Such action must be penalized as 'holding'.

4   *Obstruction* Whilst the obstruction law is generally well understood and applied, the following are aspects where lack of uniformity is apparent:

4.1 *Playing distance* This is determined by whether the player concerned *can* play the ball at any given moment *if he wishes to*; if the ball is beyond his control in terms of distance and he is preventing his opponent from playing it, then he commits the offence of obstruction.

4.2 *Charging from behind* A player who obstructs his opponent but commits no offence because the ball is within his playing distance may be charged from behind. This means a charge in the region of the shoulder, but not in the back itself; any kind of charge near the spine is obviously very dangerous and is forbidden in all circumstances.

5   *Offside* If the ball is in play and has been last played by or has touched an opponent before it reaches a player in an offside position, this player cannot be given offside. This is laid down in the law. Referees are advised that when the ball is played forward to the zone of play where a player is in an offside position, they should whistle immediately and not await the outcome of the pass.

Other Considerations

6   *Use of advantage* When a referee refrains from whistling for an offence it is important that he should indicate clearly by voice and gesture that he is using 'advantage' so that everyone may know that the offence has not escaped his notice. The use of advantage does not absolve him from the responsibility of dealing with the offending player at the first opportunity if the offence deserved disciplinary action, for failure to take such action often leads to retaliation from the offended player.

7   *Dropping of the ball* Referees are reminded that 'dropping the ball' means holding it at waist level and removing the hand so that the ball drops to the ground; it should not be thrown down in any way.

8   *Penalty kicks*

8.1   The player taking the penalty-kick must remain inside the penalty area or ten-yard arc until the signal is given for the kick to be taken; after the signal he may then go outside the arc in order to take a longer run at the ball, though he cannot demand that opponents give him a clear path to do this.

8.2   A player taking the penalty-kick may try to deceive the goalkeeper as to his intentions, and such action is allowed. This is quite different from 'trickery' when the player stops his kicking action in order to make the goalkeeper move in one direction, and then kicks it in the other. This is quite contrary to the spirit of the game and the player at fault should be cautioned and the kick retaken if a goal has resulted.

9   *Free-kicks* When free kicks are taken there is usually a number of players involved with no limitations imposed on the defenders except that they shall be ten yards from the ball, and free-kick situations are often tactical manoeuvres between attackers and defenders. It is therefore considered that deceiving tactics by the players taking the kick are just as acceptable as they would be in the general run of the game.

2   Specific topics

A)   OBSTRUCTION (FIGURES 14, 15 and 16)

The obstruction clause of Law 12 has remained unchanged since it was first introduced in 1951. It became necessary because of the practice, fairly common in some countries, of a player stepping in front of an opponent to block his path to the ball without making any attempt to play the ball. There was no punishment for this action until the International Board decided that it offended the spirit of the game. The offence is described as: 'when not playing the ball, intentionally obstructing an opponent, i.e., running between an opponent and the ball, or interposing the body so as to form an obstacle to an opponent.' (Law 12.3)

In chapter 10 it will be seen that obstruction of opponents can be used as a means to impede vital tactical play. It is important, therefore, to differentiate between what is fair and what is unfair when a player appears between opponent and ball.

To put the new law into its proper perspective, the FA issued carefully worded explanations of various situations which arise in match play in its Memorandum on Refereeing No. 5 of August 1951. Because the observations are still very relevant to modern football they are reproduced here with illustrations.

What constitutes the offence of obstruction?

During any match, in the ordinary course of play, there are many occasions when a player will come between an opponent and the ball, but in the majority of such instances this is quite natural and fair. He is intent upon playing the ball and is entitled to make every legitimate move to obtain or retain possession of it. Provided that the ball is within playing distance the player may interpose his body between opponent and the ball in a feint to play at it and yet allow it to go to a colleague. This is again legitimate.

It is when the ball is *not* within playing distance of a player (say two or three yards) and when he is *not* making any attempt to play the ball that this new offence *may* occur. But it is strongly emphasized, the offence *must* be *intentional*. It is quite possible for a player when not playing the ball to be in the path of an opponent and yet not be guilty of intentionally obstructing.

Common sense of officials in interpreting the spirit of the game will help to differentiate between incidents of obstruction which are fair and those which are

E

intentionally unfair. A study of the following incidents may assist in distinguishing between 'offence' and 'no offence' in the matter of obstruction:

(i)   Player A makes a pass to B (one of his colleagues) and tries to run forward to collect the return pass at A1; an opponent X, ignoring the ball, *deliberately* steps in front of A to bar his path to the ball at A1; X makes no attempt to charge, but *deliberately* positions himself to obstruct. [See figure 26.]

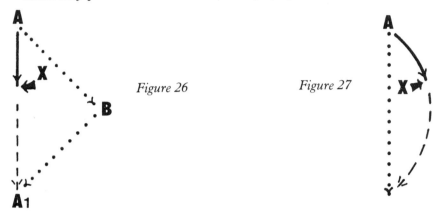

Figure 26   Figure 27

X is contravening Law 12 (2) 3 and the punishment is an indirect free-kick, taken from the place where he made the *intentional* obstruction.

(iii)   A, having beaten X by pushing the ball forward, attempts to run round him. X moves to block his path; he makes no attempt to charge A but, facing him, deliberately positions himself to obstruct A's progress. [See figure 27.]

In this case again, X is making no attempt to play the ball. The result is that he is merely preventing A from taking part in the game or from making a reasonable attempt to play the ball. He should therefore be punished by an indirect free kick from the place where he committed the offence.

It is again emphasized that this new clause dealing with intentional obstruction in no way empowers the referee to ignore the more serious offences in section 1 of Law 12. It is still a foul for a player to elbow an opponent out of the way or off the ball, just as it is and always has been a foul to hold an opponent or push him with the hands. Furthermore, these fouls are punished by *direct* free kicks or by penalty kicks where applicable, and if the fouls are persisted in, the referee has power under Law 5 (d) and (g) to deal with the offender drastically by suspending him from taking part in the game.

(iii)   The ball is running out of play either over the touchline or the goal-line. Defender A follows it for some yards, keeping the ball within his playing distance. Opponent X, chasing the ball, finds A between himself and the ball with A's back towards him. X may charge A from behind (Law 12 (e)) but A is not offending against the new clause because, theoretically, the ball is under his control, even though he allows it to run out of play.

But if A seeing the ball running out of play, deliberately obstructs X when the ball is out of playing distance then he has committed an offence penalized by an indirect free kick. [See figure 14.] Similarly, if A turns his back on the ball to face and obstruct X even though the ball is within playing distance he cannot be making an attempt to play it, therefore he is committing an infringement of the law.

(iv) A traps the ball and turns on it with it still under control. His body is now interposed between the ball and an opponent. Here A does not commit any offence because he is in possession and is within his rights in denying it to an opponent. [See figure 16.]

(v) A is receiving a pass and runs into a position so that, when the ball reaches him, he is between an opponent and the ball. This is a fair movement and there is no offence.

Decision 8 specifies that movements of the obstructing player with outstretched arms which force the challenger to change course and are intentional become an act of ungentlemanly conduct. A caution shall be awarded to the offender. The qualification, 'but does not make bodily contact', implies that if contact *is* made the offence then becomes one of holding or pushing, for which a direct free kick is the award. If the offence occurs in the offender's penalty area a penalty kick must be awarded. 'Interposing the body so as to form an obstacle to an opponent' does not always relate to the body being between opponent and ball.

Decision 9 spells out the offence of obstructing the goalkeeper, 'in an attempt to prevent him from putting the ball into play …'. The ball is now *between the two players*. It is clearly intended that the goalkeeper shall be given the opportunity of releasing the ball without obstruction but within the restriction placed on him by Law 12.5 (a), the 'four-step rule'.

There is considerable divergence of opinion and action in situations where an attacker confronts a goalkeeper who is holding the ball. Let us assume that the goalkeeper has just caught the ball (figure 28).

Question 1	What legal options are open to the goalkeeper?
Answer	(a) He can throw the ball.
	(b) He can move to gain momentum to kick the ball out of hand (within four steps).

Figure 28

Question 2	What legal options are open to the attacker?
Answer	(a) He may stay where he is (the goalkeeper may drop the ball).
	(b) If the goalkeeper stands still, he may *fairly* charge the goalkeeper (hoping that the charge will take the goalkeeper and ball into the goal).
	(c) If the goalkeeper moves, he may *fairly* charge the goalkeeper (again hoping for a goal or, alternatively, to force the goalkeeper to release the ball).
Question 3	What action by the attacker constitutes obstruction?
Answer	Any action which blocks the path of the goalkeeper in an attempt to prevent him from releasing the ball within the allotted four steps.
Question 4	Does this mean that the attacker must remain stationary if the goalkeeper moves?
Answer	No. He may move parallel to the goalkeeper but may not step in front of him.
Question 5	If the goalkeeper stands still and the attacker moves from side to side, is this allowed?
Answer	No. The attacker is clearly *intentionally* blocking the path of the goalkeeper.

Question 6	If the goalkeeper moves from side to side and the attacker follows him, is this allowed?
Answer	Yes, provided that the attacker does not *intentionally* step in front of the goalkeeper.
Question 7	If the goalkeeper gains possession and the attacker then runs to stand in front of the goalkeeper, is this allowed?
Answer	Yes, because the attacker is permitted to charge the goalkeeper when the latter is holding the ball. We then revert to the original situation.

Comment

Goalkeepers have no right to expect attackers to withdraw to allow them to release the ball. A goalkeeper always has the option, and the advantage, of throwing the ball. Attackers have as much right to the ball as goalkeepers and should be allowed *fair* opportunities to obtain possession.

B)   ADVANTAGE

In chapter 2 the 'advantage clause' of Law 5 has been described as setting aside the letter of the law to apply the spirit of the game. In addition to the examples quoted in chapter 2 there are others which relate to the taking of penalty kicks. Law 14, Decisions 3 (a), (b) and (c), allows the referee to ignore infringements by the goalkeeper (not being on the goal-line or moving his feet), or by another defender (encroachment), to avoid delaying the penalty kick and/or distracting the kicker. Similarly, an infringement by an attacker (encroachment) may be ignored (Decision 4 (b)). The result of the kick determines the action which will be taken. The principle that offenders will not be allowed to profit by their offences is clear. The spirit overrides the written word.

Law 5 (c) permits the referee to add 'time lost through accident or other cause'. One recognized cause is an attempt to waste time. The spirit of the law allows discretion in the calculation of time played so that time-wasting tactics are unsuccessful.

A defender may attempt to save a goal by handling the ball before it enters the goal. The handling offence occurred before the ball crossed the goal-line. Technically, Law 12 requires the award of a penalty kick but penalty kicks do not always result in goals. If the referee awards a penalty kick and it fails the offending team will have gained an unfair advantage. Therefore the correct award, applying the advantage clause, is a goal.

The foregoing examples illustrate clearly the practical application of the spirit of the game. During the run of play the task is more difficult. The classic example of the attacker regaining his balance after being tripped by a defender and having an excellent chance of scoring a goal is illustrated in figure 29. To stop play for the free kick or penalty kick would almost certainly be to the disadvantage of the offended team.

Figure 29   Applying the advantage rule in a situation when a goal might be scored

There are other situations which can cause much discussion among officials as to the right course of action. Basic questions on the use of advantage include the following:

1   Is advantage influenced by the timing of play?
2   Is advantage influenced by the position of the incident?
3   Does retention of the ball necessarily justify advantage?
4   When should advantage always be applied?
5   When should advantage never be applied?

These questions have been put before groups of referees of various grades and in several countries. A summary of opinion, which can serve as a policy outline, is given below:

Question 1   Is advantage influenced by the timing of play?

Opinion   Yes. A general policy adopted in practice is to resist applying advantage in the early stages of a match in order to establish authority and control.

Question 2   Is advantage influenced by the position of the incident?
Opinion   Yes. The nearer to goal the more effective advantage becomes. It is generally accepted that advantage is inadvisable when the ball is in the half of the offended team or in mid-field.
Question 3   Does retention of the ball necessarily justify advantage?
Opinion   No. An example quoted is where the ball is handled in the penalty area and falls to an attacker. Unless there is a ninety-nine per cent chance of a goal retention does not justify a play-on call.
Question 4   When should advantage always be applied?
Opinion   When a goal is almost certain to result.
Question 5   When should advantage never be applied?
Opinion   In cases of serious injury, serious foul play or violent conduct.

Advantage is frequently applied at dead-ball situations, for example, to allow free kicks, corner kicks and goal kicks to be taken quickly before the whistle has been blown and before defending players have retired at least ten yards from the ball.

The opinion expressed in response to question 1 reveals that observance of the spirit of the law is not the only consideration. Its application in the early stages or, as some referees reason, at any time during a tough game, can undermine authority and control.

Advantage situations vary from the obvious examples already quoted to others of a minor nature, which occur when it is in the interests of the game to keep the play flowing; here we revert to the appeal of Law 5, Decision 8, not to interfere by stopping play for trifling and doubtful offences. Applying advantage in minor situations must be related to the degree of co-operation and general sportsmanship of the players. It should always be applied where control has been established and the referee has good co-operation. If he senses that his control is suffering his advantage calls can be limited to the more obvious situations.

Time and space are important factors. If play is open there is more time to assess the impact of stopping the game. When several opposing players are close to the ball it is generally better to stop the game quickly. The merits of this policy are that friction between the players is likely to be less and the possible advantage situation will not be so apparent.

Communication of advantage is also important for the reasons discussed in chapter 6. Players and spectators should be left in no doubt that an offence has been seen but that play is being allowed to continue.

Once given an advantage decision cannot be revoked, as spelt out in Law 5, Decision 7. Every referee experiences situations where an offence occurs and advantage is called but the player with the ball kicks it past the goal or falls a few paces later. The temptation to return to the scene of the offence and award a free kick or penalty kick is sometimes difficult to resist because justice has not been achieved. The referee is not allowed this option.

Two final points. The first is that the application of advantage does not exempt the offending player from disciplinary action. The second is that 'The letter and spirit of Law 12 do not oblige the referee to stop the game to administer a caution. He may, if he chooses, apply the advantage. If he does apply the advantage, he shall caution the player when play stops.' (Law 12, Decision 6). The why, when, where and how of advantage can only be described here in terms of guidance. Every situation will need to be read as it occurs. How the individual referee arrives at his decision will depend on his fundamental appreciation of the spirit of the game and his knowledge of other factors discussed in chapters 8, 9 and 10.

C) OFF-SIDE

The purpose of the off-side law is discussed in chapter 2. Its interpretation requires special study because it is the only law which is concerned with the tactical formation of players when the ball is in play.

For easy reference the terms of Law 11 are quoted below in full, together with the sole International Board decision relating to this law:

Law 11 – offside
A player is off-side if he is nearer his opponents' goal-line than the ball *at the moment the ball is played unless*
(a)   he is in his own half of the field of play
(b)   there are two of his opponents nearer to their own goal-line than he is
(c)   the ball last touched an opponent or was last played by him
(d)   he receives the ball direct from a goal kick, a corner kick, a throw-in, or when it was dropped by the referee.

Punishment

For an infringement of this law, an indirect free shall be taken by a player of the opposing team from the place where the infringement occurred.

A player in an off-side position shall not be penalized unless, in the opinion of the referee, he is interfering with the play or with an opponent, or is seeking to gain an advantage by being in an off-side position.

International Board Decision (1956)

(1)   Off-side shall not be judged at the moment the player in question receives the ball, but at the moment when the ball is passed to him by one of his own side. A player who is not in an off-side position when one of his colleagues passes the ball to him or takes a free kick does not therefore become off-side if he goes forward during the flight of the ball.

The basic questions are simple:

1 *Fact*   Is the player in an off-side position at the moment the ball is played by a colleague? (Only if he is do the next questions arise.)

2 *Opinion*   Does his position influence the play or an opponent?
                or Is he intending to gain an advantage?

There are five features of this law which should be studied:

1 *Timing*
  Question   When does the judgement of fact start?
  Answer   At the moment the ball is played by a colleague.

2 *Position*
  Question   What is an off-side position?
  Answer   The player must be in front of the ball in his opponents' half with one or no opponent between himself and the goal-line.

3 *Interfering*
  Question   How can interfering be judged?
  Answer   The International Board decided in 1924 that 'if a player who is in an off-side position advances towards an opponent or the ball and, in so doing, causes the play to be affected, he should be penalized'.

4 *Seeking advantage*
  Question   How does the referee judge seeking to gain an advantage?
  Answer   By the same reasoning as applies to judgement of intention to commit an infringement.

5 *Exceptions*

Question	If a player *is* in an off-side position, when should he *not* be penalized, even though he is interfering or seeking an advantage?
Answer	When (a) the ball was last touched by an opponent or was played by him (b) he receives the ball direct from a goal kick *or* a corner kick *or* a throw-in *or* when the ball is dropped by the referee.

PROBLEMS OF INTERPRETATION

Timing

This is the starting point for the judgement of off-side. It is not the moment to stop the game because other factors must be assessed before the final decision can be made. The referee (and linesman) must freeze in his mind a picture of the disposition of attacking and defending players who are ahead of the ball at the moment it is played towards the opposing team's goal-line. Having noted that an attacker *is in an off-side position* we move to the next sequence of events and the next problem of interpretation.

Interfering

A leading coach has said that any opponent can be considered to be interfering with play simply by being on the field. He had in mind the influence of the player on tactical formations. A defender in a left-back position may have to take into account the position and potential movements of an attacker near to the opposite touchline. This interpretation is stretching the intention of Law 11 too far. The 1924 definition of interfering is quoted as a reminder of the physical relationship of the attacker to the play or to an opponent.

Further evidence of the interpretation of interference appeared in the first referees' chart issued by the FA in 1887. Under the heading of 'hints to players' the following advice was given: '... when standing off-side you have no right to impede an opponent nor to station yourself so near to the goalkeeper as to hamper his movements'. In 1922 this advice was repeated with a few words of additional clarification. After 'goalkeeper' came: 'or any other opponent as to hamper his movements or obstruct his sight of the ball'.

From these early words of guidance and the 1924 definition it is clear that 'interfering' means a close physical relationship to the ball or to an opponent in a position to play the ball. It follows that interference must be based on the direction in which the ball is played and the next zone of play. The two factors of direction and zone must be linked. This is particularly important in the judgement of off-side in the following situation, which occurs frequently (see figure 30).

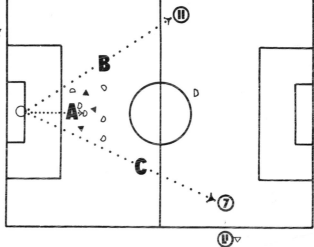

Figure 30   Off-side: interfering

The goalkeeper has the ball in his penalty area and prepares to kick out of hand. At the moment he kicks the ball colleague *7* is standing in an off-side position on the right wing. Colleague *11* is on-side on the left wing.
    Consider three possibilities:

A The ball is kicked slowly towards the near group of players. Attacker *7* is not penalized because he will not be involved in the next zone of play.

B The ball is kicked quickly towards on-side attacker *11*. The next zone will not involve *7* and he is not penalized.

C The ball is kicked quickly towards *7* who prepares to play the ball. He is penalized in this situation because he is in an off-side position and is interfering with (the next zone of) play.

    The next important factor is that *the timing of the movement of the ball influences an off-side decision.* We see that attacker *7* is in an off-side position at the moment the ball is played by the goalkeeper, but we have no idea where the ball is going until time has elapsed for its direction and length to become apparent. Linesman *L1*, patrolling the attacking half of the field, will find this situation particularly difficult to judge in terms of when to signal 7 off-side. He is often unfairly criticized in situations where the ball is played slowly along path *C. L1* correctly judges the direction and next zone of play and signals 7 off-side. In the meantime during the flight of the ball 7 runs back and is apparently on-side when he receives it. The decision is correct, the criticism unjust.

A particular incident in a vital Football League match serves as a classic case in the judgement of interfering with play. At the end of the 1970-1 season Leeds United were well placed to win the First Division championship when they travelled to play West Bromwich Albion. The manner in which the game was decided led to intense publicity and television debate when one of the West Bromwich goals was hotly disputed by Leeds. They claimed that a WBA player should have been judged off-side.

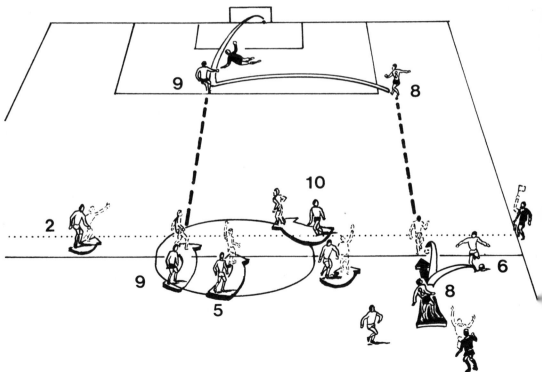

Figure 31   West Bromwich Albion v Leeds United 1971

The situation is illustrated in figure 31. Leeds no. 6, Hunter, in possession just inside the opposing half, attempts to pass the ball inside to a colleague. The pass is badly executed and the ball strikes WBA player no. 8, Brown. At this moment no. 10, Suggett, is standing in an off-side position in the Leeds half. When the ball hits Brown it rebounds several yards ahead. Brown collects the ball and runs towards the Leeds goal-line. The linesman raises his flag to indicate Suggett's off-side position but referee Tinkler waves play on. Brown advances to the edge of the Leeds penalty area, passes the ball across to Astle no. 9, who scores easily.

The Leeds protest was based on the claim that when the ball rebounded off Brown, Suggett was interfering with play. Referee Tinkler, well placed to assess the situation, decided correctly that there was no pass intended by Brown towards Suggett and that Suggett was not involved in the next (immediate) phase of play. The goal was allowed, Leeds lost the match 1-2 and ended the season in second place to Arsenal. The margin was one point.

Seeking to gain an advantage

Should Suggett have been penalized for off-side under the clause of 'seeking to gain an advantage'? It may have been in his mind that he should remain in his position to take advantage of a counter-attack. The facts were that when opponent Hunter was in possession, moving into the WBA half, Suggett was walking back towards his own half. Then the unexpected rebound from Brown occurred. In Tinkler's opinion Suggett's intentions were innocent. Had he been placed *behind* Hunter and had the ball travelled in his direction close enough to bring him into the next zone of play, he might have been judged to have been interfering but not seeking to gain an advantage.

The difference, then, between 'interfering' and 'seeking' is that the first must be measured by the physical relationship between player, ball and opponents and the second on his intention of being in a certain position.

'Played on'

Exception (c) in Law 11 causes much debate in the interpretation of a defender being the last player to touch the ball when an opponent is in an off-side position. There is no problem when the defender is in possession and, say, passes the ball back towards his goalkeeper not realizing that an attacker is in a position to intercept. The attacker is not off-side (figure 32A).

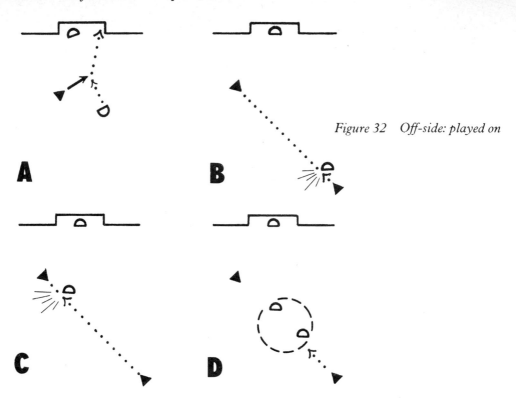

Figure 32   Off-side: played on

The problem arises when the ball is passed towards the attacker by a colleague and a defender attempts to play it and suceeds in touching it, but it continues to the attacker (see figure 32B). At the moment of the pass the attacker is potentially off-side. Potentially, that is, from the point of view of the timing of the ball leaving the foot of his colleague. We have seen that, before interfering can be assessed, the direction of the pass and the next playing zone must be considered. The next playing zone could be where the defender is if he obtains possession from the pass. It would be incorrect to penalize the attacker for off-side now. The play has entered a new phase. The same applies when the defender touches the ball but does not prevent it from reaching the attacker. However, if attacker and defender are in close proximity, C, the next zone of play is where they are. The attacker is now interfering and should be penalized.

A time factor applies to the judgement of played-on. In B the timing of the change of the phase of play is short because of the proximity of the kicker to the defender. In c it is longer and the referee will be able to signal when or before the ball touches the defender. In practice it would appear that referees are inconsistent because some will allow play to continue after the ball is touched, B, while others will stop play when the ball is touched in c. But it is not necessarily a question of inconsistent refereeing, simply that the time scale must be taken into account.

The two examples examined here are the extremes. It is when the defender is about mid-way between the two opponents that inconsistencies appear, D. In an attempt to achieve uniformity of action FIFA have given the following guidance:

'Having decided that a player is in fact off-side, the referee should blow his whistle immediately and not await the outcome of the pass. If, however, the ball touches, or is played by an opponent, whilst he is going to blow his whistle (but has not already done so), he should not blow it. (The action of the ball touching or being played by an opposing player brings into effect the 'unless' clause and referees are not entitled to ignore it.)

Chapter 13 includes some specific off-side examples.

Summary

Uniformity in the interpretation of the laws is of universal importance, particularly now that video recordings of top-level matches are distributed to many countries. The subject appears in the programme of every coaching course for referees.

From time to time certain aspects of interpretation need review because of trends in the tactics of the game. Developments of a localized nature appear and become so widespread that a reappraisal is necessary. One example is the tackle from behind which develops from a slight increase of physical contact to warn the opponent of the presence of the challenger, to violent body impact.

Official memoranda are issued as reminders of what is intended in the practical application of the laws. A few films are also available. In particular, FIFA's *Towards Uniformity of Interpretation*, a 16-mm colour film, deserves special mention. Other films are listed in the bibliography.

This chapter summarizes various official interpretations and has discussed three major topics in some depth so as to provide a co-ordinating guide for present and future match officials. Some interpretations remain as valid today as they did when first set down many years ago.

5 Systems of Control

Previous chapters have been concerned with the background, basic principles and interpretations of the laws. How can this knowledge be put to good use on the field of play?

The referee's first duty is to enforce the laws. Armed with a whistle and a licence to blow it there should be little problem here. The laws should be known by the players. It should only be a matter of blowing the whistle to stop the game, putting the ball in the correct position, indicating which team should have possession and then signalling the restart of play. If only it were that simple!

Basically there are three factors which influence the manner in which a referee controls a football match: 1 – personality, 2 – system of control, and 3 – technique. After a few observations on personality, this chapter concentrates on systems of control as practised and as outlined in official instructions and advice. The new referee is urged to study official requirements in detail. They provide the framework for practical match control. In later chapters actual match play situations will be presented with suggestions on how to improve individual technique and standard of performance.

PERSONALITY

Why should personality have any bearing on the way a match is controlled? It is one thing to be given authority, but it is quite another to exercise that authority in such a manner that instructions are accepted and carried out without question. Personality implies personal authority or personal influence. The individual with a strong personality is likely to impose more authority and discipline than one lacking in personal distinction. One of the pillars of personality is conviction: conviction that what is being done is right. Conviction is an attribute which all referees have in common.

How does an individual achieve the ultimate in personal influence over others? A big question which politicians have tried to answer for centuries. There is no exact answer because every individual is his own man, conditioned by environment and by the influence of others. No words written here will change the past environment of a reader. However, we can try to help the reader to make reasonable assessments of the factors which apply to his own personality and suggest how to develop it. One of these factors is confidence – confidence based on sound knowledge of the theory and practice of match control. Personality and confidence are discussed in more detail in chapter 8, but it can be stated here that a referee who lacks a strong personality can be as effective as a more fortunately endowed colleague by acquiring a thorough knowledge of the game and efficient match control techniques.

SYSTEMS OF CONTROL

Throughout a referee's career different systems of match control will be required according to the assistance available. It is almost certain that the following degrees of assistance will be experienced:

a) none, that is, the referee will be alone
b) one non-qualified linesman
c) two non-qualified linesmen
d) two qualified referees acting as linesmen.

a) The sole official

Many matches, particularly the first at junior level, must be controlled without assistance. The referee has total responsibility for all decisions. Mistakes will certainly be made but most players and team officials will accept that a sole official will be unable to monitor every situation, for example, the ball momentarily crossing a boundary line some distance from the referee. It is usually enough for the referee to seek the co-operation of the players before the start of the match in a friendly and polite manner.

Moving around the field to remain in contact with the play will require a good level of fitness. Hints on reaching and maintaining a satisfactory level are given in chapter 8.

Judgement of off-side situations will probably be the most difficult task for the lone referee. It is certain that occasions will arise when it will be physically

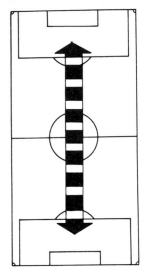 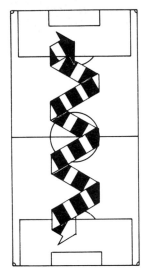 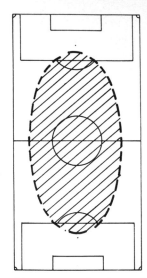

Figure 33a   Straight-line patrol   *Figure 33b   Zig-zag patrol*   *Figure 33c   Oval patrol*

impossible to make on accurate judgement, for example, when the ball is cleared quickly from a corner kick to an attacker in the other half of the field. If there is any doubt the benefit should be given to the attacking team. A loud and confident call to 'play on' may help to convince the defending players that the correct decision has been made and so reduce the probability of appeals.

There are three systems of patrolling the field which can be recommended for sole control. They are:

1   straight-line patrol
2   zig-zag patrol
3   oval patrol.

1   STRAIGHT-LINE PATROL

A useful guide for the new match official is to adopt a straight-line patrol for his first few matches. This involves moving along an imaginary line drawn between the two penalty marks (figure 33a).

Most junior football is played on fields which are close to the minimum dimensions. Following the straight-line patrol will mean that the referee will be about twenty-five metres from each touchline, and providing that touchline markings are reasonably visible he should not experience too much difficulty in judging ball-out-of-play situations. The main advantage of the straight-line patrol is that the referee can take the shortest path, about seventy metres, to reach the penalty areas. This gives the inexperienced official a little more time to make judgements on off-side situations and incidents in and around the penalty areas. The use of this patrol should encourage mobility and discourage the bad practice of trying to achieve control without moving out of the centre circle.

2   ZIG-ZAG PATROL

As experience and confidence are gained the patrol can be extended to a rough zig-zag (figure 33b): Variations from the straight-line patrol will become appropriate as the official moves with the area of play up, down and across the field. He will then obtain a closer view of incidents and will not need to sprint too far when play switches quickly from one side of the field to the other.

3   OVAL PATROL

Depending on the mobility of the referee a further system of patrol will be possible. This will involve covering a larger area in the shape of an oval (figure 33c).

   This patrol will put the referee in closer contact with the play and will enable him to avoid being isolated to the corner areas. Common sense will dictate when it is advisable to vary these guidelines. For example, if the centre of the field is very muddy it is a simple matter to adjust the patrol so that difficult areas are avoided. With all three systems the referee will need to move to the goal-line to monitor corner kicks. It is generally advisable to adopt a position near to the furthest goalpost from the ball.

b)   Referee plus one non-qualified linesman

When a volunteer can be found to assist the referee, to act as a linesman, the recommended system of patrol is the linear system modified. This is a variation of the straight-line patrol.

4   LINEAR SYSTEM MODIFIED

Figure 34 illustrates the referee's line of patrol on a straight line but to one side of centre. The assistant patrols the opposite touchline and indicates when the ball is out of play over the touchline or goal-lines.

The advantages of this system are that the play is in front of the referee most of the time. He can monitor touchline situations on his side of the field while remaining within reasonable contact of incidents in the space between the penalty areas. A side view of off-side situations is another advantage. To be successful the system calls for good mobility on the part of the linesman. If the referee observes that the linesman tends to remain near the halfway line he must adjust his patrol so that he moves into the centre at the penalty areas. See dotted lines in figure 34.

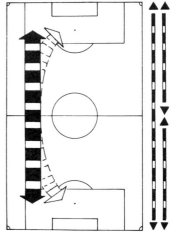

Figure 34   Linear system

c) **Plus two non-qualified linesmen**

The availability of two assistants, who are probably members of the two clubs involved in the match, becomes more usual as the referee is appointed to control more important matches in junior football. One of two systems is normally chosen to patrol the field with two assistants – either the linear system or the diagonal system.

5   LINEAR SYSTEM

The linear system is the same as that illustrated in figure 34, except that the two assistants patrol one half only of the touchline opposite the referee.

Most referees, however, adopt the diagonal system as described below.

d)   **Plus two qualified linesmen**

As the referee progresses he will be provided with two qualified referees to assist him as linesmen. He will then be required to adopt the Diagonal System of Control.

6   THE DIAGONAL SYSTEM OF CONTROL

Due to the rapid growth of international football it became necessary to consider the best method of controlling match play and to impose one system throughout the football world.

The official system, which was first introduced by Sir Stanley Rous when he refereed the FA Cup Final of 1934, between Manchester City and Portsmouth, is the *Diagonal System of Control*. Every referee must be fully conversant with its theory and its application.

Three officials are required to supervise play. The theory is that the referee patrols diagonally across the field while each linesman supervises one half of the field from the touchline. Figure 35 shows the imaginary diagonal line of patrol for the referee and the touchline patrolled by each linesman.

The object of the system is to achieve the most effective co-operation between the three officials by keeping the immediate area of play between two, i.e., the referee assisted by the linesman in the half where the play is, while the third is positioned to cover quick break-away movements into the opposite half. Figure 36 illustrates the point. When the play is at *A* the referee is on the left, supported by Linesman *L1* on the right. Linesman *L2* is abreast of a potential off-side situation should the ball be transferred quickly into the other half. Similarly, when play is in the vicinity of *B* the referee has moved along his diagonal to *RB* and Linesman *L2* is assisting.

The successful application of the system depends upon two basic factors:

1   Intelligent positioning of the referee and his linesmen.
2   Complete co-operation between the three officials.

For a number of given situations (e.g., a goal kick, a corner kick, free kicks in mid-field) basic positions for the three officials are recommended in diagrams published by FIFA in its excellent booklet *Laws of the Game and Universal Guide for Referees*, and by the FA in the *Referees Chart and Players Guide to the Laws of the Game*.

A detailed analysis of positioning, in the use of the diagonal system in

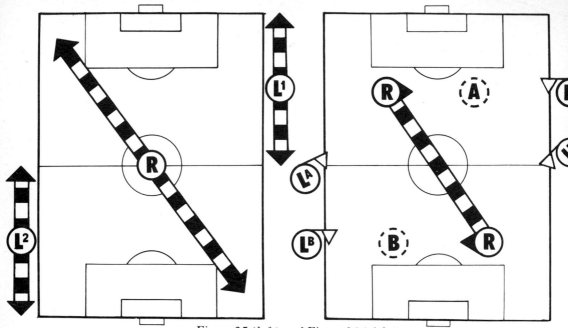

Figure 35 (left) and Figure 36 (right)

practical match situations, is included in chapter 7. Additional comments, on the manner in which the system should be used to assist in reading the game, are included in chapter 8.

In its Memorandum on Refereeing No. 5, dated August 1951, The Football Association gives the following advice:

> Normally, efficient control can be exercised by keeping roughly to a line from the corner of one penalty-area to the opposite corner of the other penalty-area, a distance of about 85 yards. When compared with the full distance between the corner-flags, of about 125 yards, it will be seen that to cover the shorter distance only entails quite a substantial saving in energy. It also means, particularly on a holding surface, that the referee is more easily able to reach the vicinity of play.

Co-operation between referee and linesmen

Law 6 requires linesmen to '... indicate when the ball is out of play and which side is entitled to the corner kick, goal kick, or throw-in. They shall also assist the referee to control the game in accordance with the laws.'

The degree of further assistance is left to the discretion of the individual referee. In practical match control there are many ways in which linesmen can assist the principal official.

A referee, who is provided with two assistants, whether they are club volunteers or formally appointed neutral officials, will find his task greatly eased if he gives careful thought to the manner in which he proposes to use their services.

Club Linesmen

A distinction must be drawn between the degree of responsibility delegated to the club volunteer and that accorded to a qualified neutral official. For example, the referee is instructed '... to act upon the information of neutral linesmen with regard to incidents that do not come under the personal notice of the referee.' [Law 5 – Decision 11].

Specifically, in the same Law, Decision 5, the referee is expected to cancel a goal if a neutral linesman reports on an incident which occurs prior to the scoring of the goal, provided that he (the referee) did not see the incident. This degree of responsibility must not be delegated to a club linesman.

The quality of co-operation which can be experienced from non-qualified linesmen varies according to the enthusiasm and interest of the individual. A player who has been left out of his team at the last moment, and has been pressed into service when he would rather go home or be doing something more interesting, may not be of much help. On the other hand there are many club followers, and administrators, who are pleased to take an active part in the game and will observe the instructions of the referee to the letter.

One of the early assessments of the referee is the extent to which he can rely on the co-operation of his club linesmen and adjust his own patrol during the run of play. It should soon become apparent whether a linesman is moving intelligently along the touch-line, and is concentrating on the game, or is more interested in carrying on a conversation with friends grouped near to the half-way line.

In general, instructions to club linesmen include the following:

1   The touchline which each linesman is to patrol.
2   Which team's forwards he should adopt, i.e., those of his own team or the opposing forwards.
3   To indicate when the ball has completely crossed the touch line and to indicate which team is entitled to the throw-in.

4   Signal when the ball has crossed the goal-line for a goal kick or a corner kick.
5   Check that the ball is correctly placed inside the goal area for a goal kick.
6   Stand near to the corner-post and indicate if the ball goes out of play from a corner kick.
7   Signal if a player is considered to be in an off-side position but to discontinue the signal if the referee does not agree that Law 11 has been infringed.

All other matters will be decided by the referee and at all times the referee's decision must be accepted as final without any form of dissent.

Provided that these, or similar instructions, are given clearly, and are acknowledged, during a brief pre-match conference, the possibility of misunderstandings can be reduced to a minimum and useful co-operation may be anticipated.

The thoughtful referee will include a pair of linesmen's flags in his bag, to encourage club volunteers to give clear and accurate signals.

Neutral Linesmen

Neutral linesmen must be used as assistant referees.
This is the official advice to the referee, when he has the services of two neutral officials who are qualified referees. The match is then under the supervision of three officials although the referee retains the ultimate authority and responsibility for overall control.

As previously noted, neutral linesmen can in effect act as referee in special circumstances, by bringing to the notice of the senior official acts of serious misconduct, or important incidents which the latter has not seen.

During the development of the game as a highly competitive sport the need for closer surveillance of play has become more necessary. The role of the neutral qualified linesman has advanced to the stage where he is truly an assistant referee and not merely an official waving a flag to impart information of a purely routine nature.

The minimum requirements of co-operation between the Referee and his assistants are that he shall inform them on the following matters:

1   The time by his watch.

2   The side of the field which each linesman will patrol in each half of the match.

3   Their duties prior to the start of play, e.g., inspection of goalposts, nets and flagposts.

4   Which shall be the senior linesman in case of need.

5   Positions to be taken at corner kicks.

6   The manner in which he will acknowledge the linesmen's signals and over-rule if necessary.

7   Duties in supervising throw-ins, e.g., whether to concentrate on the thrower's feet or hands.

Other items, which have become fairly standard, include the following;

8   *Timing* The referee may require neutral linesmen to indicate by a pre-arranged signal how many minutes remain for play in each half.

9   *Entry into the field of play* There may be occasions when special assistance is needed from linesmen, when they may enter the field of play; their duties should be discussed in advance. It is usually advisable for entry only:

   a)   to render assistance when the referee is injured,
   b)   to prevent an escalation of misconduct between players which may arise in the linesman's immediate vicinity.
   c)   to ensure correct placing of the ball and possibly to supervise encroachment at free kicks awarded close to the linesman's touchline. This action should only occur after the linesman has received a signal from the referee.

10   *Off-the-ball incidents* Linesmen should be told what is required of them if incidents occur which the referee is unable to see. Incidents of serious foul play, violent conduct or misconduct likely to bring the game into disrepute should be drawn to the referee's attention without delay.

11   *Signals* It is essential that the referee understands the signals of linesmen. A guide to linesmen's signals is included in chapter 6.

12   *Off-side* The linesmen's role in judging players in off-side positions is vital to good control. How the referee and linesmen co-operate should be discussed before every match. Linesmen must be instructed on positioning to monitor off-side when the ball is in play and also at dead-ball situations, e.g. to keep in line with the second rear most defender, except when the referee instructs a linesman to move to another position.

13 *Substitution* The linesmen's duties in the supervision of substitutions and recording of information (e.g. identities of players involved) should be established.
14 *Misconduct* Linesmen may be asked to record certain facts which will assist the referee, during and after the match, e.g., details of misconduct and identities of persons involved.

A referee and two neutral linesmen are, effectively, the third team at a match. The degree of understanding and co-operation they achieve will have an important bearing on the efficiency of control and enjoyment of play.

Summary

To run haphazardly all over the field, following the play without experienced assistance, is inefficient and too demanding physically. To remain in the centre circle is not so demanding but is even more inefficient. Referees must have a system of control which puts into practice as effectively as possible the theory of the game and its laws.

Several systems of control have been discussed in this chapter. Each has its advantages and disadvantages. The choice of system will be influenced by the degree of assistance available. The systems are as follows:

a) Sole official:
   1 *Straight-line system*
   2 *Zig-zag*
   3 *Oval*
b) Referee plus one non-qualified linesman:
   4 *Linear-modified*
c) Plus two non-qualified linesmen:
   5 *Linear*
   6 *Diagonal*
d) Plus two qualified linesmen:
   6 *Diagonal*

Co-operation between the referee and his linesmen in the operation of the diagonal system has been covered in some depth. Other factors of co-operation between officials are discussed in the following chapters.

⑥ Communication

Clear communication is essential to good control. Having made a decision the referee needs to make his views known to the players so that the correct action is taken and the game proceeds with the minimum of interruption. What guidance is available to enable information and instructions to be conveyed clearly to all concerned? The laws are unhelpful. Law 5 (i) simply requires the referee to 'signal for recommencement of the game after all stoppages'. The law does not state how to signal. Nor is there reference to the use of a whistle until we read International Board Decision 8, which mentions 'constant whistling for trifling and doubtful breaches'.

Law 13, Decision 1, is more helpful: '(1) In order to distinguish between a direct and an indirect free kick, the referee, when he awards an indirect free kick, shall indicate accordingly by raising an arm above his head. He shall keep his arm in that position until the kick has been taken.' The FA included the following guidance in its Memorandum on Refereeing No. 4 of November 1949:

> The giving of signals and signs is the chief method of controlling the game and should, therefore, be clear or plainly visible. The whistle is the recognized signal by which the game is stopped. It should have powerful and distinctive sound and should be blown loud and long enough to be heard above other noises connected with a match.

Also: 'The referee can, where necessary, show the purpose of his decision in stopping the game by simple gestures, e.g. touching his hand when the offence is handling.' The same memorandum comments on signals between the linesmen and the referee.

This chapter deals with communication in two sections: 1) communication by the referee, and 2) communication from the linesman to the referee. The subject of linesmanship is discussed at the conclusion of 2.

1   Communication by the referee

The whistle, hand signals and gestures are the means of communicating. When and how?

The whistle must always be used to stop the game when an infringement has occurred. It is not necessary to sound it in certain obvious situations for example, when the ball is kicked high over the crossbar by an attacker. Nor is it necessary in practice to whistle the restart at a goal kick or a throw-in. A simple wave of the hand is enough.

The whistle should be reserved for doubtful situations, for example, when the ball momentarily crosses a goal-line or touchline and returns into the field. It should be used to start free kicks and corner kicks.

How the whistle is used will reflect the thoughts, personality, authority and determination of the referee. He should make the whistle talk. A short, sharp note for a routine restart, for example, the kick-off; a strong longer blast for a severe offence. A player who appears to be taking an unduly long time to put the ball into play from a goal kick or throw-in may need urging by two or three quick short notes.

The pitch of a whistle is important. Various tones are available. A whistle will sound different at a match played in an enclosed stadium from one played in an open park. Therefore at least two whistles with different tones should be standard equipment. Several whistles of different tones have other practical advantages; for example, where a match is played close to other matches some confusion can arise from the signals of other referees. Also, interference can come from a spectator with a whistle.

It is advisable to attach the match whistle to a thong which can then be secured to the hand or wrist by a slipknot. It is unwise to run with the whistle in the mouth – a blow in the face from a hard-kicked ball can be very dangerous. There is also the tendency to sound the whistle too quickly or involuntarily.

In a 1966 World Cup match the referee carried the whistle in his mouth. During the first half it was knocked from his mouth near the edge of a penalty area. With presence of mind he pulled out a second whistle and continued, but it was very noticeable that for the remainder of the match he was anxiously searching for his first whistle each time he found himself near the spot where it had dropped. His concentration on the match was disturbed by this incident. His control suffered.

Body language is important in communicating to others. Every individual speaks in the way he carries his body in his personal mannerisms, gestures and facial expressions. A great deal can be learned about a person without him speaking. The movements of the frame, limbs, hands and eyes of a referee disclose personality, determination, and emotional stability. A casual wave of the hand is quite the wrong signal for a hotly disputed claim for a corner kick or goal kick. A rigid arm with hand extended conveys the message in a manner which carries conviction.

OFFICIAL SIGNALS BY THE REFEREE

Although the Laws make reference to only one signal (e.g. the raised hand for an indirect free kick), other signals have become recognised as imparting useful information and are now approved by the International Board.

The signals are illustrated in figures 37 to 43.

Figure 37

Figure 38

Figure 39

Figure 37 *Play on - advantage. The signal used by the referee to indicate that play should continue, when he has seen an offence but is applying the advantage.* Figure 38 *Indirect free kick. The official signal required by Law 13 (International Board Decision 1).* Figure 39 *Direct free kick. Indicates direction of free kick.* Figure 40 *Penalty kick. A clear signal towards the penalty mark*

Figure 40

Figure 41

Figure 41   *Goal kick. Point towards the correct side of the goal area.* Figure 42   *Corner kick. Point towards the corner area.* Figure 43   *Caution or dismissal. The yellow or red card should be clearly displayed as shown, and the offender's identity recorded before play recommences*

Figure 42

Figure 43

OTHER SIGNALS USED IN PRACTICE

Indirect free kick

A slight variation to the official instruction to raise one arm to signify an indirect free kick (figure 38) has been adopted by many officials. It requires the referee to maintain the signal until the ball has been played by a second player or goes out of play. This has been found helpful when the ball has been kicked directly into goal and it has been necessary to disallow the score. The continued signal provides visual confirmation that a goal cannot be allowed and helps to reduce dissent.

From personal research involving two years' study of methods of referee communication I have found that signals other than those illustrated are used in practice:

Number of signals per match
minimum recorded	7
maximum	25
average	14

The above figures include repetitions of the same signal. An analysis of six matches produced twenty-seven different signals.

These fell into two categories:

1 *Instinctive* Natural gestures which mimed the offence, for example, pushing, handling the ball, kicking (see figure 44).

Figure 44   Instinctive signals

2 *Designed* Specific actions devised by individual referees to signify offences difficult to mime, for example, obstruction, off-side, dangerous play.

Most signals were indicated by use of hand or arm; some involved movement of foot or leg, a few the whole body. Referees who attempted to communicate appeared more decisive and efficient than those who made little effort. On many occasions it was clear that negative player/spectator reaction was stifled when a firm, clear signal was displayed.

Sometimes when play was stopped and the referee did not clearly indicate the infringement, irritation and confusion arose and officials were unfairly criticized.

PROBLEM SIGNALS

Play on/advantage

Most referees use the same signal for 'play on' (there is no offence) and 'advantage' (offence has been observed but continue) (figure 37).

It was particularly evident on several occasions that the 'advantage' clause of law 5 was applied excellently but the signal was misunderstood. Spectators and players out of range of a verbal indication of advantage assumed that the referee had missed an obvious offence. Unfair criticism followed.

Designed signals

Devised by individual referees, these signals attempted to inform players and spectators of infringements other than those for which a simple gesture would suffice. 'Advantage' was one. Some were able to convey the intended message, others were unclear.

Time allowance

Few players and even fewer spectators are aware of the referee's policy in making allowance for 'time lost through accident or other cause' (Law 5). There is no official signal which allows him to indicate that he is adding one, two, or more minutes to elapsed time.

In certain South American countries the referee raises an arm and extends the number of fingers equivalent to the minutes he is allowing. The signal is given clearly to the linesmen, and for all to see, at the end of the half in which time has been lost and when the ball is out of play.

In one European cup match played in England the referee stopped play at the end of forty-five minutes, signalled one minute time allowance, and then restarted play by dropping the ball. This procedure is quite incorrect. In another match, between West Bromwich Albion and Liverpool, the display of a recognizable time signal might have saved the referee from a very unpleasant experience. The home team were in sight of an unexpected victory with the score at 2-1, when Liverpool equalized in the third minute of a three and a half minutes' time allowance. Home team supporters blamed the referee for the disappointing conclusion and promptly assaulted him. The referee was of the opinion that the extra minutes were fair compensation for time lost in the second half through trainers' visits to attend injured players, fans invading the field and time-wasting tactics. But he was unable to inform players and spectators of the amount of time allowed.

On average during a normal match there are over one hundred stoppages for goal kicks, throw-ins, corner kicks, free kicks, goals and injuries. Total time lost can vary between twenty-five and thirty-five, minutes, but only exceptional stoppages for injury, time-wasting and the like are timed for allowance. It seems sensible that the referee should indicate when exceptional delays are being timed if for no other reason than to communicate to all that he is alert to time-wasting tactics.

CONCLUSIONS

Signals demonstrated firmly and clearly in a dignified manner aid match control. In addition to the official basic signals referees need to communicate other information by using simple gestures which mime the offence. The use of the same signal for 'play on' and 'advantage' is confusing. Officials are subject to unfair criticism arising from misunderstandings. Certain offences, for example, obstruction, are difficult to mime. A variety of personalized signals have been devised which are likely to be unfamiliar and are in need of co-ordination. An indication of timing at exceptional stoppages seems desirable.

There is a growing body of opinion which considers that football needs a code of signals which imparts more specific information and reduces the element of confusion and which will improve communication between the referee, the players and the spectators. Football is a long way behind in this respect; other sports have established signal codes in their rules of play. The following table demonstrates the point:

G

	Official signals		*Official signals*
cricket	8	basketball	18
volleyball	10	rugby league	39
hockey	13	football	1

Perhaps the main reason why football law has not been orientated towards communication is because the laws have always been designed for the playing of the game. A century ago legislators could not have foreseen a situation in which over six hundred million people would be able to enjoy watching from their own homes the pleasures of the final of the World Cup tournament.

It seems unbelievable that just one man, the referee, should be the only person to know the exact reason why the game has been stopped, but the official memorandum must be followed until the governing authorities agree that a code of signals is needed.

2   Communication between the linesman and the referee

In the previous chapter the point was made that the success of controlling a match under the diagonal system depends on the degree of co-operation between the referee and his linesmen.

OFFICIAL SIGNALS BY LINESMEN

The officially approved signals by linesmen are illustrated in figures 45 to 51. Four signals relate to off-side, and one each to throw-in, corner kicks and goal kicks.

Figure 45   Off-side. Flag held vertically

Figure 46   Off-side. After play is stopped, linesman indicates position as appropriate, on the far side of the field...

Figure 47 Off-side. ... or in a central position...

Figure 48 Off-side. ...or on the near side of the field

Figure 49 Throw in. Linesman indicates direction of throw

Figure 50 Corner kick. Linesman points to corner area, after checking that the referee has accepted ball-out-of-play signal

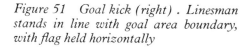

Figure 51 Goal kick (right). Linesman stands in line with goal area boundary, with flag held horizontally

OTHER LINESMEN'S SIGNALS USED IN PRACTICE

All signals by linesmen are solely for the information of the referee. It is expected of referees that signals be acknowledged whether action, for example in the form of a free kick, is to be taken or not. The third team has to be seen to be working together. If it is necessary for the referee to over-rule a linesman his signal to the linesman should indicate friendly acknowledgement but polite refusal. The linesman should never be made to appear foolish.

Linesmen may be required to assist the referee by indicating time remaining and when time has expired in each half. Some referees ask for a signal at any time during the last five minutes of each period, others only when the period is complete. Football League officials signify time expired by placing one arm across the chest (figure 52a).

Figure 52   Time signals

The number of minutes remaining can be signalled by extending the appropriate number of fingers against a contrasting background, for example against the linesman's flag or uniform (figures 52b and 52c). Such time signals are for guidance only. The referee remains the official timekeeper.

Confirmation of the position of an infringement in or near the penalty area may be required when the referee is unsure. If inside, some referees ask for the flag to be placed across the chest. It is then not necessary for the referee to consult verbally with his linesman.

Official advice stresses the point that there shall be no unnecessary use of signals and that the use of the flag shall be reduced to a minimum. When a signal is given it shall be specific and clear.

3   Linesmanship

Signals of information are only part of the duties under the heading of co-operation between referee and linesmen described in the previous chapter.

Linesmanship is a subject in itself. The sooner a referee obtains experience of running a line the better will be his awareness of the problems of linesmanship. For example, a linesman is unable to get very far away from the distractions of a hostile crowd close to the touchline. It is too much to hope that spectators will agree with the signals of linesmen when decisions are given against the team they favour. Criticism and abuse from close quarters are likely to be experienced by every linesman. This is unfortunate enough, but the referee should be on the look-out for situations where linesmen are likely to be subject to more than verbal taunts, and be prepared to take action to protect his colleagues.

It may be necessary to change the diagonal at halftime or at any time for the sole purpose of reducing interference with a linesman's patrol. The encroachment of spectators on and over the touchline where there are no restraining barriers, the throwing of missiles, and even climatic conditions may pose such severe problems for linesmen that efficiency is seriously affected.

At all times the referee remains the principal official. He should never abdicate his responsibility for the final decision, as occurred in the following incident. During an international tournament in New Zealand a goal was scored. The defending captain ran to the referee claiming that an attacker was off-side. Instead of making the point that he had decided the goal was good and ending the matter, the referee invited the captain to speak to the linesman. Thus encouraged, the captain, joined by two vociferous colleagues, ran to the linesman and engaged him in animated argument while the referee calmly waited in the centre circle.

'Neutral linesmen must be used as assistant referees' means that the referee who takes the trouble to achieve a good understanding with his colleagues before a match will receive the degree of assistance needed to control the game in a proper manner.

Linesmen should be encouraged to undertake several important preliminary duties such as:

1   checking field dimensions and equipment with the referee
2   checking players' equipment, for example, footwear
3   checking team colours and reporting to the referee irregularities with competition rules.

During the pre-match discussion linesmen will be advised on a number of basic requirements concerning positioning. The referee will inform linesmen of the diagonal he intends to use and positions to be taken during corner kicks.

Other requirements which have become fairly standard practices include the following:

1   If unsure of the direction of a throw-in the linesman will raise the flag directly above his head. The referee will indicate the direction and the linesman should then point his flag to signal the decision in a confirmatory manner.

2   Face the field when giving flag signals, holding the flag in the appropriate hand and away from the body to indicate direction. (This can mean changing the flag from one hand to the other and is preferred to placing the arm across the body.) Figure 53 shows the same signal as in figure 49 but in the opposite direction.

3   If there could be some doubt about the direction of a throw-in when the ball crosses the touchline near the goal-line in the other half of the field, the linesman should check whether the referee is in a better position to judge. If so, the signal procedure should be as in 1.

4   When incidents are observed which can affect the result of the game or which constitute serious foul-play or violent conduct and which have not been seen by the referee, the linesman shall wave his flag immediately and maintain the signal until acknowledged (figure 54).

Figure 53

Figure 54 A linesman reports an offence by an attacker which he has noticed just before the ball entered the goal

5   The flag must be carried open, not furled around its stick.

6   It is not necessary to wave the flag to signal a goal unless there is some doubt; for example, the goalkeeper may carry the ball over the goal-line into the goal. If satisfied that there is no problem a movement towards the halfway line will be understood by the referee as a 'silent' signal.

7   Positions at:
Corner kicks Move quickly to a position on the goal-line, at or near the corner post (to check encroachment when the corner kick is on the linesman's side). After the kick, resume position on the touchline without delay, cutting across the corner of the field if play permits, while continuing to face the play.
Goal kicks Check position of ball and that it passes out of the penalty area direct from the goal kick.
Free kicks by attacking team After receiving a signal from the referee, move to the goal-line to take up a position as for corner kicks.
Off-side Remain in line with the second rearmost defender unless otherwise instructed.
Goalkeeper clearances Check goalkeeper carrying the ball outside the penalty area.

Practical hints for linesmen

While the role of a linesman is subordinate to that of the referee it should be approached with the same enthusiasm and attention to detail. The following hints are based on actual incidents, some of which were quite embarrassing at the time:

1   Check that the flag is securely fixed to its stick. If it is not it can fly off at the worst possible moment.
2   If of short stature, remember that it is a real possibility that you may tread on the flag when holding it towards the ground.
3   Check carefully the touchline you will patrol for dips, hollows or obstructions which might cause you to fall.
4   Most movement along the touchline is by sidestepping and running backwards. Include these movements in your physical training programme to reduce the possibility of muscle strain.
5   Carry the flag in the hand which is hidden from the referee. This avoids flag movements being mistaken as signals. The nearest hand is then visible to give discreet signals of information such as 'play on, no off-side' to the referee when he looks for assistance. There may be occasions when the referee prefers to have the flag visible at all times, for example, when the match is played in poor visibility or under floodlights. Check which method is preferred.

6   Avoid running on the touchline if possible, to reduce damage to the line. If there is a path or athletics track close to the touchline consider how to avoid inadvertently stepping on the edge. You could twist an ankle.

7   Carry normal accessories as if you were the referee, that is two watches, notebook, pencils, coin, whistles. You may be called upon to take over the match without warning. Synchronize your watches with the referee before the match. If you are the senior linesman you may be required to make time allowances as if you were the referee, so that you have an accurate indication of time remaining should you take over the match.

8   Keep a record of the game, as if you were the referee: times of kick-off, goals scored, team colours, shirt numbers, and some description of players cautioned or dismissed. The referee may require assistance with one or more of these points later, and if you do take over you have an accurate record.

9   Check objects and people on the far side of the field for possible confusion of colours with the players. Ball boys, vendors, stewards, and photographers may present a clash of colour at a vital moment of the match. Similarly, a substitute warming up on the far side may be taken as a player if his normal playing colours are visible.

10   Watch carefully for off-the-ball incidents and draw the referee's attention to serious offences. Warn the referee at halftime if you think he has not observed off-the-ball friction developing between certain players.

11   Follow the ball to the goal line on all occasions to be in a good position to judge in- or out-of-play situations.

12   Watch for goalkeepers who add illegal reference marks to the field when the referee is otherwise occupied.

13   Do not engage in conversation or argument with players or spectators.

14   Always include two clean linesmen's flags in your kit (for the use of club linesmen) to replace dirty or torn flags provided by the home team, or to be produced in the absence of flags.

15   Assist the referee as you would wish to be assisted if you were in his position.

Summary

The study of an expert traffic director can be a lesson in the art of communication without the use of the voice. Instructions and information flow in a series of carefully designed and well executed movements of hands, arms, trunk, head and eyes and facial expression. Add a whistle to simulate an extension of the voice and the communications system is almost complete. This is what is required in an expert referee: the ability to convey the message with the minimum of signals.

The voice has an important role in the control of a match, perhaps more particularly in the control of certain players. A quiet word of advice, information or warning can be the equivalent of many non-verbal signals for offences which the receiving player may have committed. Verbal control is to be preferred in this situation, but so many messages have to be transmitted at long range. A clear visual system of communication is therefore essential to efficient match control.

Official signals, few and simple, have been described and illustrated. Others of an instinctive nature are used in practice by every referee. Some are personalized signals designed in the absence of an official standard method. In contrast to the signals of the referee those of the linesman are purely for the information of one person – the referee. Official requirements have been illustrated.

The subject of linesmanship has been discussed both in the sense of communication with the referee and in the technique of performance. As experience is gained in running the line certain refinements of technique will develop. Observation of others will help to develop good and eliminate bad techniques.

"He's rehearsing — in charge of the United versus City game this afternoon"

7 Practical Match Control

This chapter is devoted to an analysis of actual match play situations. It is structured to encourage the reader to analyse and to draw the right conclusions when confronted with similar situations on the field of play. When analysing the spirit within the law in chapter 2, a key word was used to question the meaning of written law. To analyse match control it is helpful to adopt a similar approach. The first task is to find the key to practical match control.

The key to practical match control

Let us analyse the process which every referee must use to tell players and spectators that he is stopping a game for an infringement of the laws. Working backwards, the process is as follows:

Action the signal to stop play, that is, blowing the whistle

Decision the result of a thought process involving the measurement of the incident against the referee's understanding of the laws

Observation registering the incident through the medium of the eyes.

The first point, elementary of course, is that seeing the incident (*observation*) is necessary before we can weigh up the arguments for and against (*decision*) and make a signal (*action*). But this process can only start when the referee is able to see the incident; and he will only be able to judge what he can see from where he is.

The key to practical match control is, therefore, to be in a *position* to see incidents. In other words if the referee is not in the right position he cannot see, therefore he cannot decide, therefore he cannot act. And if he does not act when he should the result is inefficient match control. The quality of decisions must be influenced by good or bad positioning. How then can the referee put himself in the best position to see? Basically, every position is dictated by two types of play: 1) static play (dead-ball situations) and 2) dynamic play (mobile play). Static play is dealt with below. Dynamic play is dealt with in the next chapter.

Dead-ball situations can be subdivided into 1) fixed and 2) variable, as follows:

1   *fixed situations*
   a)   place kick
   b)   goal kick
   c)   corner kick
   d)   penalty kick
2   *variable situations*
   e)   throw-in
   f)   free kicks inside the penalty area
   g)   free kicks outside the penalty area
   h)   free kicks mid-field

Figure 55 illustrates static play situations.

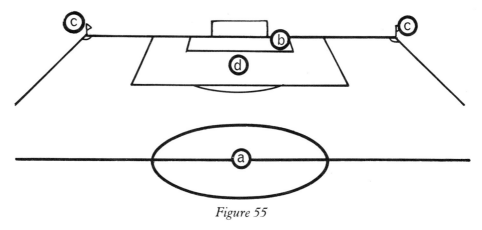

Figure 55

It is appreciated that referees have special problems when controlling matches where linesmen are club officials or, as is often the case, where the official operates without the assistance of linesmen. For the moment it will be assumed that neutral linesmen are available and that the diagonal system is in operation.

1   FIXED SITUATIONS

a)   *Place kick*

Points to be observed for correct place kicks:

i)   ball on centre mark
ii)   attacking players in own half
iii)   defenders in own half and outside centre circle
iv)   linesmen in position on each side of the field and in the correct half of
       patrol
v)   correct numbers of players, all within field of play
vi)   field clear of all but players

In practice referees have differing ideas on the best positions at a place kick.
Five of the favourite positions are shown in figure 56. There may not appear to
be much difference between these positions but if, for example, the referee has
chosen the diagonal illustrated, positions 4 and 5 would leave him well away
from his diagonal should the attacking team move forward with the ball. He
would also have his back to his first operative linesman *L1*. From position 1,
the referee would almost certainly find himself getting in the way of play if –
and this is a common move in modern football – the ball was played back to a
supporting colleague. Not a good start to a game! 2 or 3 seem to be the most
sensible positions to observe all of the foregoing points and to be clear of the
opening play.

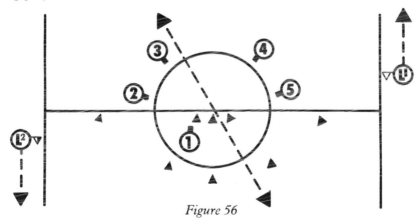

Figure 56

b)   *Goal kick*

Checklist for goal kicks:
i)   ball to be kicked from correct side of goal area
ii)   ball inside goal area
iii)   ball kicked beyond penalty area

Frequently the next area of play from a straightforward goal kick is in the region of the centre circle. Most referees seem to favour a position somewhere around the semi-circle inside the half of the field from where the kick is to be taken (see figure 57).

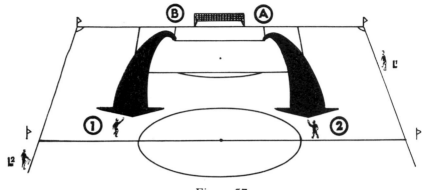

Figure 57

The object is to keep clear of the possible landing area of the ball and to obtain a side view of players challenging for possession.

When the ball is kicked from *A* a good position for the referee would be somewhere near 1. If the kick is from *B* then 2 would apply. Both 1 and 2 have the advantage of keeping play between the referee and his operative linesman. *L1* is in the referee's vision from 1 and *L2* from 2. If the referee positions himself on the same side as the goal kicks the chances are that he will cause interference to the players when the ball arrives in his vicinity. Instead of moving towards the next area of play with a side view, the referee will find himself dodging and weaving to get out of the way, thus having to turn away from the potential trouble spot. His control of the situation is then momentarily lost. This could mean missing a vital infringement.

The referee should be alert to the quickly taken 'short' goal kick, where the ball is passed to a defender colleague just outside the penalty area. In a Football League First Division match played in London the referee was not observant enough to see the goalkeeper preparing to take a quick goal kick to a colleague. An attacker was. He moved in swiftly to challenge the defender. The defender, realizing that the tactic was likely to fail, resisted the challenge by pushing the attacker. In retaliation the attacker knocked his opponent to the ground. The incident lasted no more than ten seconds. The referee was walking slowly back to the centre circle, anticipating a long goal kick. When he turned he found one defender unconscious and the goalkeeper fighting with the attacker. If he had read the 'short' goal kick he could have remained reasonably close to the penalty area and might have been able to intervene before blows were struck.

c)   *Corner kick*

Many goals result directly or indirectly from the corner kick situations. Therefore what happens at a corner kick can be vital to the outcome of any match. Because the ball is nearly always kicked into the target area, where both teams have concentrated their players, the chances of infringements by attackers and defenders are higher than at any other stage of a game. An efficient referee gives careful thought to his positioning at corner kicks so as to observe and deal promptly with incidents. From my observation, referees favour one or more of the five positions shown in figure 58. Position no. 5 is behind the goal.

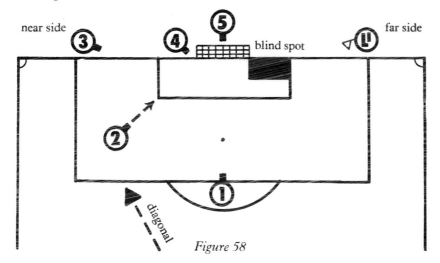

Figure 58

Check list for corner kicks:		
i)	position of ball in quadrant	iv) **infringements near goal-line**
ii)	encroaching by a defender	v) **infringements near penalty mark**
iii)	ball out of play after being kicked	vi) keeping clear of play
		vii) regaining diagonal

Position 1
Advantages of this position include a wide-angle coverage of play in the penalty area, a side view of near-post incidents and close observation of incidents near the penalty mark. Its disadvantages may include interfering with play and the view of goal-area incidents being obstructed by players. Useful for regaining the diagonal quickly.

Position 2
Not recommended for far-side corner kicks because of screening by players and the problem of judging the ball out of play. For the near-side corner it is a good initial position to observe correct placing of the ball and encroachment by defenders. Keeps the referee clear of play until the ball is kicked. A movement towards the goal area after the ball is kicked gives a close view of goal area incidents. Recommended for near-side corners only.

Position 3
Useful for dealing with (i) and (ii) at near side and for (iii) at far side, also for (vi) in both cases. However, may be too far from goal area incidents to be recommended.

Position 4
A good observation position, clear of play, for most infringements in the target area. Could be too close to see subtle obstruction, pushing or holding at the far post.

Position 5
An unusual position with the main advantage being a clear view of incidents in the goal area. A poor position for regaining the diagonal and for observing infringements near the penalty mark. It could be a useful surprise tactic to use this position once in a match to detect attacker/goalkeeper obstruction/retaliation.

Summary
For near-side corners position 2 offers advantages as a starting point followed by a move towards the goal area for close observation or, alternatively, a move away onto the diagonal if the ball is cleared quickly.

Factors other than those listed will influence positions taken up by individual referees. These include the situation of the game, blind spots caused by the formation of players, and fitness to move quickly to mid-field positions to observe subsequent play. A common failing of referees, even at international level, is to treat every corner kick as just another kick. Officials are seen to move into exactly the same positions without reading the situations. Key questions which each referee should ask himself at every corner kick are:

i)   Far side or near side?
ii)   'Long' or 'short' kick?
iii)   How many attackers?
iv)   Where are they? What are they doing?
v)   Where are the defenders? What are they doing?
vi)   Inswinging kick or outswinging?
vii)   Direction and strength of the wind?
viii)   Is linesman in position?
ix)   Now, which is my best position to observe the actions of players and signals from linesman, without interfering with play and while remaining ready to move quickly onto the diagonal?

One vital area at a far-side corner kick is the far post. Many referees stick rigidly to one position, for example, 2, 3 or 4. The result is a blind spot at the far post, as shown in the illustration. Many incidents which occur here go undetected because the movements of offending players, for example, an attacker backing into a close-marking defender or a defender pushing an attacker from behind or holding his shirt, are all parallel to the goal-line. Neither official has a side view. More often than not the view of the referee is obstructed by four to seven players. In this situation position 1 gives a good crossfire of vision by the referee and the linesman. It is worth trying. Because a high percentage of goals result from corner kicks, attention to good positioning is essential in this dead-ball situation. Tactical fouls which occur at corner kicks are discussed in chapter 9.

d) *Penalty kick*

One penalty kick can decide the outcome of an entire match. Efficient supervision is essential. Inefficient supervision is unforgivable because it is

H

probably the simplest of all dead-ball situations to supervise. Law 14 is very specific on the positioning and movement of the players. Because of its importance in the game it is worth studying the background of the law and problems observed in actual matches.

Two major points of the current law are:

i)   the goalkeeper must stand (without moving his feet) on his own goal-line until the ball is kicked
ii) all players other than the kicker must remain outside the penalty area and at least ten yards from the penalty mark.

Why should the goalkeeper be so restricted? When the penalty-kick law was adopted in 1890 the goalkeeper was allowed to move up to six yards from his goal-line. There was no restriction on the movement of his feet. In practice goalkeepers learned to distract the penalty-takers by running forward and performing bizarre gymnastics. As a result many penalty kicks did not produce goals. The law was changed to restrict the goalkeeper from advancing from the goal. Even this change proved inadequate when certain goalkeepers ran forward to the goal-line just as the penalty was being taken, gaining the advantage of momentum to save the shot. It was then decided that the goalkeeper must remain stationary on the goal-line, between the posts, and must not move his feet until the ball is kicked.

Film evidence has shown that some modern goalkeepers have become highly expert in moving from the goal-line a fraction of a second before a penalty kick is taken. Sometimes this has been enough margin to prevent a goal, and the course of a match, even a competition, has been affected by the undetected illegal movement. It is important, therefore, that the goalkeeper be closely watched.

The supervision of encroachment by other players is also vital for the reasons discussed in chapter 2, Law 13. The point is emphasized by the requirement to caution encroaching players. As with the goalkeeper, it has become a common occurrence for players to move into the penalty area or within ten yards of the ball before the kick; this needs tight supervision. From a survey of many filmed penalty kicks covering two seasons of top-level football, an alarming proportion of one in three penalty kicks were observed to be incorrectly supervised. Some examples taken from the survey are illustrated in figures 59, 60, 61 and 62.

Match A (figure 59) – International match

Penalty awarded to visiting team in eighty-seventh minute at score of 2-1. Before ball kicked, two attackers and one defender had encroached into penalty area. Ball entered goal. Penalty not retaken. Encroaching players not cautioned. Result: 2-2.

Figure 59

Match B (figure 60) – Football League First Division

Penalty awarded during first half at 0-0 to visiting team. Players of both teams encroached before kick. Goalkeeper moved before kick. Ball punched clear by goalkeeper. Play allowed to proceed. Result: 0-0.

Figure 60

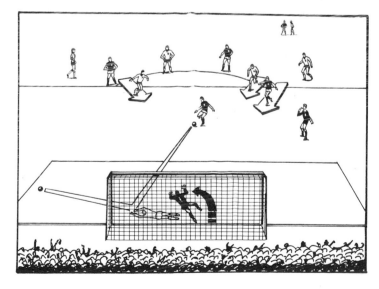

Match C (figure 61) – European Cup semi-final

Penalty awarded to home team near end of match, at 0-0. Before kick defender had encroached two yards into penalty area. Also before kick goalkeeper had moved from goal-line. Ball missed the goal. Goal kick awarded. Result: 0-0.

Figure 61

Match D (figure 62) – Scottish Cup Competition

Penalty awarded to home team at 1-1. Before kick two attacking and three defending players had encroached many yards into penalty area. Ball struck post and rebounded to one of encroaching defenders who cleared. Play allowed to proceed. Result: 1-2.

Figure 62

How should responsibility be shared between the referee and the nearest linesman to ensure that all aspects of a penalty kick are covered? A penalty kick can be analysed by considering three phases:

		Checklist		*Responsibility*
1 *Before*	i)	Position of ball		R
	ii)	Position of goalkeeper		R
	iii)	Position of other players		R
	iv)	Position of linesman		R/L
	v)	Which player is to take the kick?		R
2 *During*	vi)	Infringements by goalkeeper		L
	vi)	Infringements by kicker e.g. gamesmanship		R
	vii)	Encroachment		R
3 *After*	viii)	Ball in or out of play		L
	ix)	Infringements by kicker e.g. playing ball twice		R
	x)	Linesman's signals		R

The first five items are easily checked and appropriate action taken before the referee positions himself to give the signal and observe subsequent events. But where should the referee and linesman place themselves to obtain a clear view of items (vi) to (x)? From observation, referees choose one of the five positions shown in figure 63.

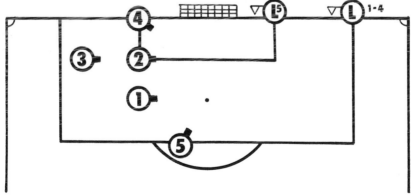

Figure 63

Position 1

This position is the most widely adopted but if the referee is facing the ball it has two serious disadvantages. The first is that it is physically impossible for the referee to watch the kicker putting the ball into play and at the same time note any players who have stepped into the area on his blind side (right rear). The second disadvantage is the natural reaction to anticipate the flight of the ball as it is kicked towards goal and consequently neglect visual cover of encroachment (right front). Several instances of serious encroachment by one or more players have been noted from filmed evidence but have gone undetected when the referee has adopted this position.

Position 2

Approximately at the corner of the goal area; referee facing the ball. This position gives a wider viewing angle and better coverage of encroachment to the right of the referee. Could be a dangerous position if the ball rebounds from post or goalkeeper.

Position 3

Level with goal-area line and near penalty-area boundary line. Provides a wide-angled view and is clear of the danger of interfering with the ball, as in 2. In certain ground conditions, for example, long grass, markings on far side of penalty area and D mark will not be visible to judge encroachment.

Position 4

At the junction of the goal-area line and the goal-line; referee facing the ball. Although further away from the eighteen-yard line and penalty arc, this position gives an even wider visual sweep and takes in the view of the goalkeeper as the ball is kicked. Keeps the referee clear of subsequent play. Recommended where the linesman is either non-neutral or unavailable. There could be a problem here with boundary markings, as in 3.

Position 5

An unusual position, but one which has proved to have several advantages, is just inside the penalty-area arc. A narrow angle of vision takes in the goalkeeper, ball, kicker and linesman, particularly if the linesman is stationed at the junction of the goal-area line and goal-line, as illustrated. The referee's presence reduces the temptation to encroach. The disadvantage is that encroachment away from the arc is difficult to detect. However, most encroachment occurs from the points nearest to the ball, that is, where the arc meets the penalty-area line. The essentials are covered from this position.

Summary

From the above observations it appears that position 1 is the least efficient. Positions 2 and 3 provide a wider viewing angle which should make for more efficient supervision. Positions 3 and 4 could be too far to effectively cover encroachment, particularly on grass fields where the markings may be indistinct. Position 5 offers a narrow angle for the essentials. When a referee does not have the assistance of neutral linesmen position 4 is recommended *after* instructing players to remain at least ten yards from the ball until it is kicked.

The penalty kick is the easiest to demonstrate on an actual field of play because of the limitations placed on the positions and actions of players. A practical demonstration using these observations as a guide is recommended to enable officials to make individual assessments of the advantages and disadvantages of various positions. The next penalty kick should then be easier to supervise efficiently.

2   VARIABLE SITUATIONS

By variable we mean that the ball is dead for a throw-in or free kick, but its position on the field of play is variable.

Variable positions are as follows:
e)   throw-in
f)   free kicks inside the penalty area
g)   free kicks outside the penalty area
h)   free kicks mid-field
Refer to figure 64.

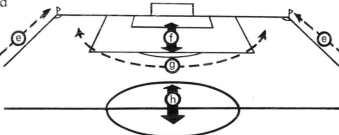

Figure 64

e)   *Throw-in*

A simple throw-in involves a minimum of fourteen points to be observed for efficient control. These are:

Before	i)	Near-side or far-side throw-in
	ii)	Correct position of throw-in, along touchline
	iii)	Attacking or defending throw-in
	iv)	Position of linesman (far-side throw-in)
	v)	Positions of players in throwing area
	vi)	Movements by players
During	vii)	Facing field
(Law 15)	viii)	Feet position
	ix)	Feet on ground
	x)	Two hands used
	xi)	Over the head
After	xii)	Ball in or out of play
	xiii)	Infringements by thrower e.g. playing the ball twice
	xiv)	Linesman's signals

The question for the referee here is, where is the next area of play? Is it likely to be towards the defending goal or upfield from a defensive position? Is the throw-in on the referee's diagonal or on the linesman's side? For an attacking throw on the referee's diagonal many officials adopt a position *outside* the touchline in advance of the thrower (see figure 65).

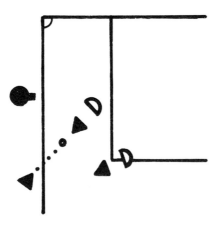

Figure 65   Attacking throw-in

This is often an excellent position because the whole of play is within the vision of the referee; he is well placed to observe off-side situations and signals of the linesman, and is close enough to supervise the throwing action without interfering with the play. An official who has not yet tried this position should be certain he is fit enough to move quickly back onto the diagonal should the ball be intercepted by a defender and be kicked upfield.

For throw-ins on the linesman's side the alert referee will move off his diagonal towards the throw and place himself slightly ahead of the thrower. He is then close enough to deal with incidents in the throwing area and yet not too far off the diagonal. Refer to diagram 10a of the diagonal system of control. Other questions which arise are: Where are the players? Are they in a formation which indicates a long or a short throw?

Some teams adopt a specific tactic when awarded an attacking throw-in near the opponents' penalty area. One player may specialize in long throws and be able to propel the ball into the goal area. Such throws are equivalent to corner kicks but have the additional element of surprise for players and officials who have not read the situation. No two throw-ins are the same. Although a succession of throw-ins may be taken from the same place on the touch line, the referee should be prepared to take up a different position each time according to his reading of the situation.

f)   *Free kicks inside the penalty area*
g)   *Free kicks outside the penalty area*

Efficient control of free kicks is one of the most vital contributions towards the maximum enjoyment of a match. Weak control of these situations can change the mood of the players and spectators. Overall control then becomes more difficult. Referees who gain the most respect and co-operation are those who adopt a calm and firm approach and ensure that the game proceeds without undue interruption.

Essential points to be observed for all free kicks can be summarized as follows:

Before	i)	Correct positioning of ball
	ii)	Attacking or defending free kick
	iii)	Positions of opposing players – ten yards
	iv)	Which player is to take the kick?
	v)	Position of linesman
	vi)	Arm signal for indirect free kick

During	vii)	Encroachment
	viii)	Infringements by kicker e.g. playing ball twice
After	ix)	Second player touching ball (indirect)
	x)	Ball leaving penalty area (defending inside area)
	xi)	Ball in or out of play
	xii)	Linesman's signals

The first essential, particularly for an attacking free kick inside or outside the penalty area, is for the referee to *arrive early* to take control. If required by the attacking team, the kick should be allowed to be taken quickly, even though defending players have not moved ten yards from the ball. It is unhelpful to the object of putting the ball into play promptly to be too pedantic about the position of the ball. Within one metre is reasonable. If the free kick is not to be taken quickly all requirements of Law 13 must be observed. The kicker should be advised to await a clear signal before putting the ball into play.

'The wall'

One common problem which all referees must handle efficiently is the defensive 'wall' formation. Most teams, having the benefit of coaching advice, are drilled to impose delaying tactics to provide time for organizing a defensive formation. Building a wall has become an accepted practice in modern football. At times referees contribute to it by not dealing quickly or firmly enough with defenders who deliberately delay free kicks. Defenders have no right to 'wall-building time'. The team offended against have every right to expect the referee to allow the kick to be taken in a manner which suits them and not the offenders. The reader is reminded of the purpose of Law 13 discussed in chapter 2. More cautions and dismissals of erring defenders may be needed to restore the balance of fair play.

How should a referee control the ten-yards requirement of Law 13? There is no standard technique. One referee will pace out ten yards from the ball; another will stand close to the ball urging defenders to move back. A few referees try to force players back physically for example, by pushing or pulling them away from their adopted positions, usually four or five yards from the ball. This method is not recommended. Field markings are useful guides to distance. In this respect the penalty-area arc and the penalty mark are natural aids.

'Be the first brick in the wall' is a useful hint when the referee arrives early on the scene of the offence (figure 66). After checking that the ball is in the correct position he moves smartly ten yards goalwards and to one side. Verbally and by gesture he then directs arriving defenders to his position.

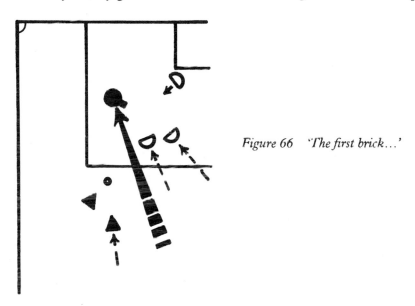

Figure 66   'The first brick…'

It is unwise to adopt a rigid technique for every match or, indeed, for every 'wall' situation in the same match. There will be occasions when unfair tactics by the attacking team need more control than delay by defenders. Moving the ball nearer to goal, pushing and harrassing defenders who have already taken up position, are actions which need firm handling. It is sometimes advisable to speak to the captain of a team which is clearly indulging in planned delaying or unfair tactics. A few words indicating that the referee is wise to the situation and will take strong action on repetition are often enough to control the problem before it escalates.

h)   *Free kicks, mid-field*

It is rare for 'wall' problems to appear at mid-field free kicks. However, a player of the offending team may move to the ball and take his time to retreat the required ten yards. An efficient referee will spot the first attempt and make it clear to the player, and others, that such tactics will not be tolerated.

Generally the referee has more space at his disposal. It is not always necessary to remain close to the position of the free kick. This is certainly true when the kicker is preparing to kick the ball a long distance, for example, into the opponents' penalty area. Here it is advisable to choose a position which gives a good view of the expected landing area of the ball and a side view of challenging players, and keeps the linesman within a narrow angle of vision. Many referees move wide on the diagonal, facing all players in the playing zone, and at the same time keeping clear of play. Refer to diagram 7 of the diagonal system of control.

Summary

Having established that *position* is the key to practical match control we have analysed positioning at static play situations. We have dealt with these first as fixed situations, and second as variable situations. In the former the ball is placed in a fixed position defined by the laws, for example, the penalty kick. In the latter the ball can be in a variable position along the touchline or within the field of play.

A consistent theme has been the warning not to become rigid in selecting positions, for example, not to treat every corner kick or throw-in as an exact replica of the last. It seldom is. Factors other than the simple supervision of putting the ball into play according to the laws can influence positioning. These factors arise from an assessment of the situation which has developed, or is about to develop, in each case. Technically this assessment is known as 'reading the game'. The skills needed for reading the game and methods of improving this vital - probably *the* most important - aspect of match control are discussed in the next chapter.

⑧ Reading the Game

Becoming efficient in choosing good positions at dead-ball situations is only part of the way towards efficient overall control. With the exception of a place kick to start or restart play, each situation analysed in the previous chapter has been the result of a decision made during dynamic play, that is, when the ball is in motion. If a bad decision is made because of bad positioning the loss of control which follows cannot be regained by superb positioning at the subsequent dead-ball situation. *The conclusion to be drawn from this fact is that the coaching of referees is inadequate if it does not include guidance on how to achieve good positions when the ball is in play.* This chapter is intended to improve the individual referee's ability to read the game and to position himself in the right place at the right time.

'Reading the game' implies that instructions are set down for each game just as a script is written for a play. Fortunately this is untrue. While every football match has components similar to a play such as a stage, players, directors (officials) and, in many cases, an audience, only an outline script is available. The actual events to take place during the first and second acts are a mystery; the heroes and the villains will not be known until the final second of the action. Every match is a unique football story. No two matches can ever produce exactly the same story, not even with identical players and officials. Despite many hours of hard work by coaches writing the script to suit their teams the outcome will always be unpredictable. For example, not even the most knowledgeable football follower would have predicted that Jack Taylor, the referee of the 1974 World Cup Final in Munich, would be required to award a penalty kick in the first minute of the match; or that a second penalty kick would be awarded to turn the fortunes of the game at a crucial stage.

The uncertainty of the game is one of its major attractions. But where does this leave the referee, the director, whose task is to control the play? How can he prepare himself to deal instantly with unpredictable events? What guidance can be given to enable him to cope adequately with his task?

First, the factors which influence reading ability will be examined and second, suggestions given for development and improvement. Some factors influence control before the game starts. The referee has to accept them as they are but he can assess their individual and cumulative affect on his match control policy. They are:

1   Predetermined factors

a)   method of control i.e. diagonal system
b)   ability of linesmen
c)   size of field of play
d)   condition of surface
e)   weather
f)   importance of match
g)   attitude of players

The following comments are not exhaustive but they should serve to provide a basis on which each official can enlarge from his own experiences.

a)   *Method of control*
b)   *Ability of linesmen*

Two important factors in controlling dynamic play are the diagonal system of control and the ability of linesmen. The latter can greatly affect the reading of a game for the reason that poor co-operation from linesmen (or the absence of qualified linesmen) throws more responsibility onto the man in the middle. More ground has to be covered to reach the desired positions to observe incidents. Instructions to inexperienced linesmen may need more detailed attention than when experienced assistants are available. It is worth recalling that the diagonal system is intended to aid control by keeping the area of play between two pairs of eyes - the referee's and one linesman's. This does not mean that with efficient linesmen the referee need only travel a straight line invisibly marked on the playing surface. A popular expression among experienced officials is, 'presence lends authority'. The closer to the incident, the better the control. There are exceptions to this but it is a good tip to follow.

Recent research in Japan produced interesting diagrams of the movements of different referees during a series of matches. Two contrasting diagrams (figures 67 and 68) underline the point of using the diagonal system intelligently.

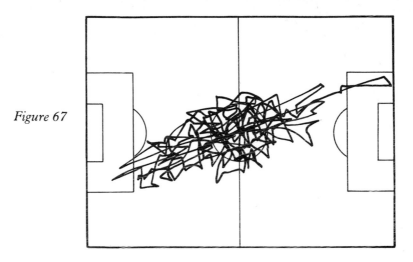

Figure 67

Figure 67 shows the path taken by a relatively inexperienced official who was also not very mobile. Note the narrow 'corridor' of his patrol and the density of movement in the centre of the field. Result – poor control.

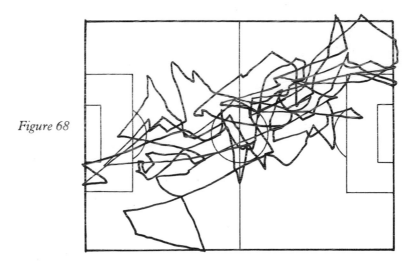

Figure 68

Figure 68 shows clearly a much more active official, an international referee renowned for his dedication to personal fitness and mobility. Note the area covered – in some cases close to his supporting linesman. Result – superb control.

The need, pointed out earlier, to avoid becoming stereotyped in positioning at dead-ball situations applies also when using the diagonal system in dynamic play. Player coaching at higher levels includes making use of the predictable referee to screen the ball from opponents. The diagonal system is intended as an aid to match control, not a rigid system to be followed regardless of other factors which may point to positions off the invisible diagonal line.

c)   *Size of field of play*

If the field is small the referee is likely to find himself interfering with play in mid-field and he may have to consider adjusting his diagonal by remaining nearer to the touchlines. More goal-area incidents are likely because of the shorter distance the ball has to travel between the goals. The smaller playing area is likely to mean more off-side problems because the 'interfering with play' and 'seeking to gain an advantage' clauses will be more difficult for the players to avoid.

On a large field the referee will need more assistance from linesmen with calls for off-side at quick breaking movements; in placing the ball at free kicks close to linesmen; in dealing with encroachment at these free kicks and controlling touchline coaching.

d)   *Condition of surface*

The nature of the playing surface, that is, whether it is wet, dry, soft, hard, level or uneven, will influence the choice of footwear and the size of studs or bars to be worn to achieve optimum mobility.

If the field has an uneven slope from one corner diagonally across to another, it may assist control to run the same diagonal across the slope throughout the game rather than running with and against the slope. Where the field slopes sharply but evenly from one end to the other difficulty will be experienced in reaching the up-side half at quick breaking movements, and the referee will need more assistance from the up-side linesman. A very wet surface will often require particular alertness to play situations because players will have problems in maintaining balance and in the timing of tackles.

e)   *Weather*

An obvious influence not always taken into account is the likely effect of the direction and strength of sun, wind or rain.

At a Football League First Division match played on an early summer evening the referee made no allowance for the position of the sun. He chose a diagonal which meant that he looked directly into a low and brilliant sun. In the opening minutes he missed two vital penalty-area signals from his linesman while blinded by the sun's glare. He had an extremely difficult match after these incidents.

It is generally advisable to run directly into a low sun so that the head is turned to observe the play. The effect of the sun's position during later stages of the game should be assessed before deciding which diagonal to run.

A strong wind blowing between the goals will affect positioning at goal kicks, free kicks and kicks out of hand by goalkeepers, and may incur delay in retrieving the ball. A spare ball kept near the down-side goal may be a wise precaution. If the strong wind is across the field more touchline incidents are likely to occur on the down side. It could be advisable to station the more experienced linesman on this touchline.

f) *Importance of match*

Every match should be important to the referee but some matches are more important than others. The first junior cup match will be as important to a new referee as the first international match is to the official of many years' experience. An extra check over pre-match factors will help towards starting with complete confidence.

Take nothing for granted – even routine matters normally left to others. Remember that the start of the 1974 World Cup Final was delayed because corner posts were not in place. An important European tie at Highbury, the home of Arsenal, was played with both teams wearing identical coloured stockings. Ball boys provided for a World Cup qualifying match in Portugal wore colours which clashed with one of the teams.

These and many other experiences confirm the wisdom of taking that little extra care with the preliminaries to a big match.

g) *Attitude of players*

Players' attitudes before the kick-off will be conditioned by many influences, for example, domestic problems, unhealed injuries, previous encounters between the teams, coaching instructions, team tactics. Factors such as these will also contribute to the degree of control needed from the referee.

The list may look formidable to the new referee but experience gained in

I

facing actual problems and mistakes made by misreading the signs will illuminate certain problem areas, and in time these will become automatic reading points for future matches. With keen observation and an intelligent analysis of these and other factors which arise before the moment of blowing the first whistle, the referee will walk into every match with the confidence that he has the situation under control and is thoroughly prepared for the unscripted ninety minutes which follow.

"Talk about a needle match — even the REF'S wearing gloves"

2   Factors within the control of the referee

Reading factors which are within the control of each referee and can be developed are:

a) knowledge
b) experience
c) psychology
d) mobility

A)   KNOWLEDGE

i) *Knowledge of the laws*

Constantly review each law and international Board decision.
Keep up-to-date with law changes, usually announced each July.
Study FIFA World Cup memoranda.
Plan and organize a personal library of published works on the game.
Discuss problem laws with others, for example, the 'advantage' clause.

Knowledge of the laws is clearly of vital concern to the match official but it is an error to assume that, once you have qualified, further study is unnecessary. The laws change and, although the changes are seldom of a major character, the referee who wants to be efficient will make it his business to keep up-to-date with the changes announced by the International Board.

There are various sources for this information. Each national authority is required to notify players, coaches and referees of new points of law, whether incorporated in the written law, published in the form of International Board decisions or as official answers to specific match problems. Details are usually made known through regional authorities but the most effective source is the local referees' association where referee coaches will explain obscure points and where debate with other officials will highlight the probable consequences of law changes in practical match play. A valuable source of practical advice is the memorandum prepared by the FIFA Referees' Committee for the conduct of the final stages of the World Cup championship. The first memorandum was prepared during the course of the 1966 World Cup in England. It provided guidance on a day-to-day basis for the thirty-one officials employed in controlling thirty-two matches within twenty days. Further information about this tournament and developments that resulted from the 1970 and 1974 series appears in chapter 11, contributed by Ken Aston.

A personal library is a must for the official who is keen to increase his knowledge of the game. Historical works on the beginnings of the modern game, as touched on briefly in chapter 2, provide a deeper understanding of the laws. They cover such subjects as the origins of the laws; the practical problems in play which led to changes; experiments with new versions of the laws. Books written by referees will include many practical experiences of value. Readers will find a list of suitable books in the bibliography. In addition, weekly and monthly magazines will keep the reader up-to-date with movements within the game, discussions on law applications by players, coaches and others. From time to time articles appearing in the press with a special interest in match control will be worth extracting and filing away for quick reference.

Discussing problem laws with colleagues is clearly an excellent method of extending knowledge, not only on points of law: in the process of such discussions the referee learns about his own attitude to the game. Specific topics on which regular discussion is necessary are the 'advantage' clause of Law 5, off-side, and practical interpretations of unusual types of fouls or misconduct related to Law 12.

ii)   *Knowledge of play*

Watch other matches live or on film or television.
Study the positioning of officials at dead-ball situations and when play is mobile.
Note recurring problems particularly at free kick and corner kick situations.
Study 'wall' formations and problems of control.
Note unusual variations of delay tactics when taking free kicks.
Note the changing character of the match relative to the score.
Note the influence of touchline coaching and the methods used.

Having played the game is an ideal preparation for the role of referee. Apart from providing experience of the basic skills, the attitudes of players and movements during a match will be better understood and will help the referee to read match play situations. When the referee is not officiating there is much for him to study and learn by watching other matches whether he is on the touchline, in the cinema or in an armchair in front of the television.

The positions of officials at dead-ball situations are easy to observe and assess. When the play is in motion it takes a conscious effort to drag one's attention away from the flow of play and towards the positions taken up by the three officials. And it is more difficult to assess when watching matches on film or television because officials are not always within the picture frame. Nevertheless, there is nearly always some point of interest for the keen official who uses his knowledge of play to search out the relationship between the play and those in control. The previous analysis of dead-ball situations in chapter 7 should be a useful framework for observing the variations of play.

The changing character of a match affects the decision-making requirements of match officials. Weather will influence the game, particularly if starting dry and finishing wet; the changing score will promote different degrees of urgency in the players; the introduction of substitutes, injuries to key players, the interchanging of positions – all will have some influence on the pattern of play and can be studied with interest while watching other matches. It is also of interest, and can be very enlightening, to glance occasionally at the trainer or coach stationed at the touchline to note how coaching instructions are given and the effect on the individual players in terms of closer marking of opponents, stronger tackling or positional changes.

iii)   *Knowledge of skills*

> Study the basic playing skills of balance and control.
> Note mannerisms, for example, those of one-sided players.
> Note methods of screening the ball.
> Note mannerisms in jumping for the ball by goalkeepers and by other players.
> Note the handling techniques of goalkeepers.
> Note the use of the arm in natural balance and when pushing an opponent.
> Observe the rate of acceleration, change of pace and direction.

Knowledge of skills enables the referee to read that much better the intention of players in their handling of the ball and to anticipate the next move more accurately. As with knowledge of play, it is useful to have played the game to know how basic skills are acquired and what is needed in terms of balance and control to carry out manoeuvres with the ball.

Some players are 'one-sided', that is, they favour either the left or the right side of their bodies to control the ball. There are many world-class players who fall into this category. The apparent handicap of not being 'two-footed' has been overcome by such players by the use of exceptional balance to manoeuvre the ball onto the favoured side. The manner in which a player positions himself relative to the ball will sometimes give the observant referee a clue to the next action, for example, the direction of a pass, a screening movement or a shot at goal. The simplest tactic in dealing with goalkeepers who favour one foot for the kick out of hand is for a forward to place himself in such a way that the goalkeeper is forced to use his non-favoured foot to clear. He is then often unable to direct the ball as accurately as he would have wished (see figure 28).

Apart from using this knowledge to watch for infringements such as the forward obstructing or the goalkeeper pushing, the referee will be better able to judge the likely destination of the ball for his next positional movement.

Knowledge of methods of screening the ball will facilitate accurate assessment of body movements by the player who has the ball within playing distance and the opponent challenging for the ball. Unfair tactics by the player in possession, such as handing off, could, if allowed to go unpunished, provoke the opponent into pushing or kicking the screening player. A recent trend in the modern game is the growing use of a hand or arm to fend off opponents (figure 69). In many instances this is done fairly, using the arm as a cushion to reduce the impact of an oncoming opponent. However some players, while apparently intent on controlling the ball, will extend the hand or arm and push the opponent. The difference is not always easy to detect, particularly when a player fends and pushes in one movement. An experienced observer will learn to judge the fairness of movements of this type.

Figure 69

The mannerisms of players in jumping for the ball are important in 'centre-half versus centre-forward' situations. In most cases the centre-half is a tall player. Many tall players appear awkward when jumping for a high ball and may be unfairly punished for what is for them a natural movement. On the other hand there are tall defenders who unfairly restrict the challenge of an opponent by extending their arms over the other's shoulders – in effect, holding him down (figure 70). Then there are forwards who appear to jump for the ball when their intention is to jump into the opponent (figure 7). Alternatively they may make little attempt in making contact with the ball but back into the opponent (making a back) so that the opponent appears to be unfairly impeding (figure 71). To pick out the player who has a natural awkward action in jumping from another who intentionally impedes his opponent it is helpful to study actions when the former is not under pressure from an opponent.

The speed and acceleration of players are worth studying. During an important cup final a small player demonstrated an exceptional rate of

Figure 70   *Figure 71*   *Making a back*

acceleration and speed when running with the ball. In the first half he beat his opposite number several times, leaving him standing. The referee, a very experienced official, failed to make use of this knowledge when, early in the second half, the same player received a long ball out of defence and prepared to dribble past his opponent. The referee was near the halfway line and the action was about to take place near the penalty area. The attacking player again succeeded in passing his opponent with exceptional acceleration, and headed for the penalty area. Another defender prepared to meet the attacker just inside the penalty area on the referee's diagonal. The danger signs were there for all to see but the referee did not increase his own acceleration and speed to keep within reasonable distance of the player with the ball. He was thirty yards behind play when the attacker was tripped. Was it inside or outside the penalty area? The referee, in doubt, judged the incident to be outside. This point is also connected with the mobility of the referee, discussed in (d).

To round off these brief comments on players and their skills, we reproduce below an extract from the 1974 World Cup report describing the characteristics of one player:

Johan Cruyff has unique physical attributes: a lean powerful frame with long legs. Like all elusive forward players, he possesses fast muscle, capable of quick reaction and contraction. He can stop and start more quickly than opponents which gives him scope to avoid a tackle, dodge past a player and race or outjump him to the ball. His endurance enables him to work incessantly throughout the game, moving first in attack then in defence, dribbling to create an opening or running off the ball to help a colleague. Then he is gifted with high skill in techniques, deft in his ball control and sensitively accurate in his passing. He is everywhere getting involved in the play, taking corners and free kicks, and then positioning himself away from the ball to create a diversion as a start to a new phase of play.

B) EXPERIENCE

i) *Quantity of experience*

It has already been stressed that experience will provide reference points to which in-play situations can be related in order to achieve good positions. The quantity of experience, in terms of the number of matches in which the official participates, is clearly fundamental to the learning curve. Officials who seek every opportunity to referee as many matches as is practicable will improve reading ability more quickly than those who control the occasional organized match. Small-sided games, five- or six-a-side, practice matches, kick-about games, all have their value as sources of match points to add to the store of knowledge.

ii) *Quality of experience*

Quality of experience will, in most cases, depend on the area in which the referee lives. In some it will be very limited. In others, particularly in large residential centres, the range will cover schools competitions through to professional football. Where it is possible to serve more than one competiton the new referee is advised to broaden his experience by applying to serve, say, one schools, one youth and two junior competitions. As the official learns and demonstrates his ability it will follow that he will be qualified to participate in more senior football and move up step by step to officiate at the highest levels of the game.

In the context of quality of experience, it is essential to gain experience of higher levels of football by serving first as a linesman. Valuable knowledge will be gained looking at match situations from a different vantage point. In addition, being a linesman provides opportunities to meet and observe more senior officials in action and to discuss the particular incidents that occur during the matches served.

iii) *Own experience*

The most difficult task in assessing one's own performance is to be objective. It is too easy to blame others for problems which have occurred. In some instances this may be valid, but on reflection it can be that many incidents have been directly or indirectly influenced by one's own shortcomings. At the end of each match, preferably when the excitement of play has cooled down, a few notes of analysis will not only serve to judge the standard of performance during that game but will also provide points on which further study and effort are needed to improve future performance.

It is not always easy to remember exact moments of play because of the speed of movement, the intensity of factors to be read simultaneously and the unknown outcome of a particular piece of play. However, a start can be made by trying to relate important decisions to the positions from which they were taken. Each goal is a reference point. Ask yourself simple questions such as:

Where was I when the goal was scored?
Was I in a good position to observe the play immediately before the ball entered the goal?
Did I check with my linesman before signalling the goal?
Was there any protest from the defending players?
What was the nature of the protest, for example, off-side?
Could I have been in a better position to be certain my decision was right?
If so, what can I learn from this problem?
Was I too far away from play, too close to play, too far ahead or behind?
Would my decision have been better accepted if I had been in a better position?
Where would that position have been? Was it possible for me to have been there? Why was I not there?

Similar questions can be applied to the positions from which penalty kick, off-side, free kick and corner kick decisions were given.

What problems were experienced with players, club officials, spectators? Consider problems which arose with individuals and others involving several people. What was the nature of each problem? How did it arise? Did I observe clearly the source of the problem? Could I have been better positioned?

Problems with linesmen: disagreements on direction of kick or throw-in. Was I at fault? Why? Did I agree with all off-side indications? If not, why not? Was I in the best position to confirm or deny? Did the linesmen carry out my instructions? If not, were my instructions clear? Can they be improved?

Did I have any problems when the ball was put into play from goal kicks, corner kicks, free kicks and throw-ins? For example, did I find myself interfering with play by taking up a bad position? Have I experienced similar problems? What can I do to find a solution?

Objectivity can be increased if it is assumed that there is at least one learning point in every match and that the analysis is directed towards finding the problem from which the point arises. It is likely that several learning points will be discovered in the process. No one official can ever be perfect. It is refreshing to hear referees of many years' experience, at the very top level of the game, admitting that they are still learning the art of match control.

iv)   *Others' experience*

Learning from others is a lifelong experience. Learning what should not be done is often given more emphasis than learning what should be done. In many instances this is just as valuable because the advice is based on mistakes committed by others, sometimes at considerable personal expense. Objectivity applies as much here as in the previous section. A person who is prepared to admit that he made a mistake is worth listening to because he is being objective and is prepared to accept possible ridicule in order to help others who might make a similar error. Seeking out such match officials will be rewarding for the inexperienced referee. A great deal can be learned in a short time by discussing practical match incidents with them. As mentioned in chapter 3, one hundred per cent accuracy is impossible, but the referee needs to work hard to reduce the incidence of error in his decisions. That the decision of the referee is final, as stated in Law 5, is as it should be in the interest of sportsmanship. It does not mean that the decision is always correct.

We have seen that the key to efficient decision-making is position. Knowing about mistakes of positioning is part of the way towards knowing the better positions. Some top officials have voiced concern that at certain stages of play they have found themselves in bad positions. For example, in the application of the diagonal system the referee sometimes finds himself interfering with play. He may be struck by the ball or impede players. The diagonal system itself is often blamed but, more objectively, the referee has not read the signs accurately or has not been mobile enough to keep clear of play. He has not taken into account the size of the field of play; the effect of wind, sun and surface condition on the tactics of the teams; the skill (or lack of skill) of the players - any one of which could have been the prime cause of his problem. Tactical fouls on the referee could also be a possible cause - see chapter 9, item 15, p.160.

'Ball-watching' is another reason why referees find themselves in bad positions. As we have seen in chapter 2 when discussing the magnetic attraction of the ball, there is a sound psychological basis for following the movement of the ball. Players' coaches have to work hard train ball-watchers to resist their natural instincts and to concentrate on the movements of colleagues and opponents when the ball is in flight. Similarly, a referee who has problems keeping clear of play should consider whether he is slow in moving to better vantage points because he has concentrated too long on the ball.

Noting trends in matches can be helpful to good positioning. In my personal experience a fairly regular pattern appeared over many professional matches. The most difficult period to control appeared about ten minutes after the start of the second half and lasted about fifteen minutes, that is, between fifty-five and seventy minutes. The reasons why this should be so can be related to the discussion on law 7, duration of the game in chapter 2.

Figure 3 (page 33) indicates how activity is likely to vary during the progress of the two periods of play. The peak period develops about ten minutes into the second half. At about this time the two teams have expended much effort in trying to impose the tactics decided upon at the halftime coaching session and are beginning to become frustrated or anxious. Tempers can become short and the referee has to be at his peak of alertness to deal quickly with signs of rough play or unfair tactics. He needs to read the signs accurately enough to be near at hand when trouble appears, if he is to keep firm control of the rest of the match.

Exchanging experiences of 'gamesmanship' must add to knowledge and alert the referee to situations which can change moods, patterns of play and positional demands. The subject of 'gamesmanship' is dealt with in some detail in the next chapter.

C) PSYCHOLOGY

i) *Own psychology*

Your psychological make-up and personality will directly influence your actions on the field of play. Your attitude to the game will also bear directly on the manner in which you deal with incidents. We have already discussed what football means to you in chapter 1. It is also true that others will react according to the way in which your actions impose on their approach to the game.

Studying their reactions will provide a mirror to your own mental approach. For example, to treat all players as criminals is to invite criminal reactions. To treat them as human beings is to invite responsible human behaviour; this is a sign of mutual respect and confidence which is observed by the vast majority of players. When major incidents have occurred in a match it may not always be entirely the fault of the individuals concerned. An analysis of the build-up to such incidents may indicate flaws in your own attitude. For example, were you being dictatorial or arrogant? Did this spark off a chain of inflammatory events? An official with an exaggerated idea of his position in the game will be blind to signs of ill temper caused by his overbearing and objectionable personality. He will find himself out of position when emotions overflow and be required to take more strict action than would have been necessary if his attitude had been less unyielding.

Psychological preparation for a match is as important as ensuring that you have packed your boots. An international level referee due to officiate at an important First Division match realized that he had left his kit at home after driving for an hour. He returned, collected his bag and rushed to the stadium. By the time of the kick-off he had expended much nervous energy and was not mentally prepared for his task. Within the first few minutes his positioning was badly at fault and two fouls were allowed to go unpunished. He never recovered full control of that match.

Psychological preparation begins the moment the match appointment is received, even though the match may be days or weeks ahead. No matter how unimportant the match may be it is a commitment in your diary and in your mind. Going through the preliminaries of exchanging correspondence with the club, planning the route to the stadium, preparing and packing the match kit, will increase the nervous anticipation of the test to come, just like the build-up to an examination. If any factor, such as the unfortunate incident mentioned above, should break down the degree of mental preparation, the referee who appreciates the value of being in good psychological condition will attempt to regain lost ground before the kick-off.

Self-confidence is a variable mental condition. It is extremely rare for an individual to remain self-confident for an indefinite period for the simple reason that the factors which make up self-confidence are variable. Knowledge of the game, of match control, is never complete. The referee can never be sure that he will be able to cope with an entirely new experience. Obviously, the more knowledge an official accumulates the greater will be his confidence to meet new situations. Physical and mental conditions vary according to such factors as environment, state of general health, domestic or business problems, and affect the level of self-confidence at any given moment.

In positional judgements during play the level of self-confidence will be an important factor. A hesitant official with a low level of confidence will have great problems in finding the right positions because he will need more time to decide. An official with a high level of confidence will quickly decide where he has to be and will move unhesitantly to that position with the knowledge that if it should need adjustment he has the mental alertness and the confidence to make the right assessment.

What can be done to achieve a high level of self-confidence before a match? First, it is helpful to analyse personal variations of confidence during normal daily life, to which the study of biorhythms is becoming more widespread in its practical application. Every person has a physical, emotional and intellectual cycle which can be charted. Charts are based on an individual's birthdate and the theory that cycle periods are 23 days for physical, 28 days for emotional, and 33 days for intellectual variations. Experts can predict fairly accurately the good days and the bad days of the cycle. In Japan long-distance lorry drivers have been the subject of close studies to determine the days when it is safe for them to drive and the days when their biorhythm chart indicates that they could be dangerous to themselves and to others. Driving schedules have been slanted towards putting them on the road at peak performance levels and giving them a day off at low chart levels. Some coaches are using biorhythm charts when preparing athletes for personal best performances. Perhaps in future, match officials will be similarly prepared.

Without knowledge of the science of bio-chemistry, the match official can assess his own variations by noting the good days and the bad and analysing some of the reasons why one day seems to be better than another. Over a period of several weeks a personal chart can be prepared which gives an idea of the individual's bio-cycle and some of the contributing factors to the good and the bad days. With this knowledge the match official is better able to prepare himself psychologically for his daily life and for the task of controlling a highly exciting and emotional football match.

Second, attention to personal grooming will be well rewarded by the added self-confidence which comes from being aware that a neat and tidy appearance attracts interest and respect. Low spirits on a bad day can be lifted by taking extra care in preparing your appearance which, when you arrive at the match, should be pleasing and dignified. It should be borne in mind that a referee represents not only himself but his colleagues and the football authority which has appointed him to the game. Several national authorities, recognizing this, provide match officials with distinctive and dignified day clothes. When three officials travel abroad to fulfil engagements they appear as a team, not as three individuals. They also reflect the respect which their national association has for their role in football. They represent their country, not themselves.

ii) *Others' psychology*

Essentially the match official's task is to control people. The point was made in chapter 3, when introducing the subject of crime in football, that the match official's role is concerned with the proper conduct of those who take part in the game. To carry out this task efficiently it is necessary to have some idea of the make-up and the psychology of other people, to recognize types and to know what motivates them. Understanding people is halfway towards managing them. Understanding players is halfway towards being in the right position at the right time to manage a situation on the field of play.

We have seen in the section on predetermined factors that the attitude of players before the kick-off is conditioned by many influences. As the referee you will not know that the small, innocent-looking number 7 of the red team had a violent argument with his fiancé just before arriving for a match and is looking for the first opportunity to express his inner frustrations, or that the goalkeeper of the blue team remembers that the ache in his left ankle is the result of a deliberate kick received from the reds' number 9 in a previous encounter three weeks previously. However, the alert official will quickly recognize symptoms in these players which suggest that their psychological condition is unstable. It may be necessary to adjust positions during the run of play to be close at hand should they lose control of their emotions. A word of advice to cool down offered at the right psychological moment can be enough to keep such players out of trouble and the match under sensible control.

It is said that personality changes with environment. How true this is can be observed in thousands of ways at a big match. The small, harmless, timid man in the street is transformed into a dancing, shouting, demoniacal extrovert inside the football stadium.

So often, players who have aggressive attitudes on the field of play are perfect gentlemen away from it. The referee has to deal with personalities as they present themselves on the field, not with what he may know them to be in normal daily life. There are many stories of referees who have found it necessary to dismiss players who are great personal friends - an interesting confirmation that the referee puts his love of the game before his love of a friend.

"It was when his team went up to collect the Cup, sarge — he picked me up in his arms and gave me a kiss"

Practically all players are motivated by the simple enjoyment of kicking a ball about, by the desire to express themselves through their skills and to experience the healthy pleasures of physical exercise. They enter the field looking forward to a good match. As we have seen this simple ambition can be frustrated according to the environment in which the game is played. It is the duty of the referee to do all within his power to control the environment so that a sporting contest ensues.

It is natural for players to express their feelings when a goal is scored by their team. The environment will dictate the manner in which these feelings are expressed. It may be unseemly for grown men to hug and kiss each other after a vital goal is scored, but it is understandable, in the same way as our quiet friend in the street will give vent to his feelings in the different environment of the stadium. Conversely, reactions to vital goals scored against are often excessive, particularly if players see the possibility of a reprieve because of a supposed infringement by the opponents before scoring. Such excesses of emotion are accepted up to a point. The referee has to judge the moment when they go beyond reasonable bounds within the context of each match, and to take whatever action is necessary to restore equilibrium. It is often the case that a quick but firm word is enough to break the glassy stare in the eyes of an over-excited player and bring him back to earth.

First, then, the referee needs to be aware of the different personalities with which he will be faced during play; second, he must recognize

"I do hope my little lecture isn't boring you, Jones"

symptoms of psychological instability; and, third, put himself in a position where he can exercise a calming or, if necessary, a disciplinary influence

D)   MOBILITY

Strictly speaking mobility is not a reading factor. It is the means of putting into effect the results of the reading factors previously discussed. Without excellent mobility the hard work of assessing reading factors will count for little. For example, assessing a situation from his deep *knowledge* of the game, learned from long *experience*, using first-class understanding of the *psychology* of the players, the referee may decide to move his position forty metres to the right. But if his mobility is poor, it may not permit him to reach the right position at the right time to observe the anticipated incident, and the result could be guesswork.

i)   *General fitness*

Good mobility stems from general fitness, a subject on which many authoritative works are available. A few simple points should suffice here to stress the need for attention to general health.

Refereeing is an athletic activity. It is common sense that any athlete who wishes to perform his activity well should begin by assessing his basic state of health, and then take positive action to improve deficiencies and develop whatever physical and mental requirements are necessary for his tasks. Questions such as, is my weight about right for my size? Do I give any thought to my diet? Am I obtaining enough sleep? may be enough to start a train of thought directed towards positive action.

Some officials feel the need for smoking and/or consuming alcohol. I do not intend to moralize about the wisdom of such habits. Simply to review current intake should be sufficient to reveal whether, by reducing or eliminating, the general state of health is likely to benefit. Adequate fresh air is clearly a must for any athlete. It is free and is the secret of a healthy blood system.

The good feeling of being healthy is probably appreciated most by those who no longer are. Those with good health tend to take it for granted until it is lost. Sometimes it is too late to recover lost health. It does no harm to stop and assess the current situation, and it could do a lot of good.

ii)   *Mental fitness*

The word 'alert' has appeared several times in previous descriptions of referees. Psychological preparation has been touched on in the last section. An alert, active mind is essential for good refereeing because visual problems are being fed into the brain at high speed. As was stated in chapter 7, in the section

K

on practical match control, the process of registering a situation through the eyes – for example, the positions, and movement of players at a corner kick and the direction, height and speed of the ball – is followed by the measurement of the action against the referee's understanding of the laws, the balancing of the answer with a tactical situation (possible advantage), the formulation of a course of action and the transmission of signals from the brain to the body to carry out that action. All in a split second.

How can an official improve mental alertness? Attention to the previous comments on general health is the starting point. Checking current alertness by simple tests is the next step.

One simple test is for officials who are car drivers to describe aloud all visual information received by the eyes during a short journey, such as the general scene, kind of road, what the cars in front and behind are doing, what traffic is approaching, pedestrians about to walk into the road, a car overtaking. Relate this to the actions which follow the mental assessment of the situation, for example, the need to change to gear, brake, accelerate, operate indicator lights, and the many hundreds of operations which are repeated in different order thoughout the journey. The speed of assessment and the associated physical movements will give an indication of the mental alertness of the driver. One thing is certain: the driver will not be able to deliver the words quickly enough to keep pace with the mental and physical gymnastics of making decisions and carrying out the actions.

Mental alertness can be improved by increasing one's powers of observation. For example, police trainees are given brief glimpses of a number of objects and then asked to give a detailed description of as many as possible. Or describe people in a photograph – shapes, sizes, clothes worn, colours, etc. Such mental exercises can be enjoyable as well as constructive.

iii)   *Physical fitness*

What level of physical development is needed by the referee? The short answer is whatever is necessary to enable him to move around the field of play in such a manner as will keep him in close touch with a fast-moving game without undue strain.

How does a referee achieve a satisfactory level of physical fitness? There is no short answer to this question because every referee will require individual advice depending on his general state of health and existing physical capabilities. Individual training is a matter for experienced physical education instructors to plan and monitor. Where a referee is fortunate enough to have access to qualified coaches at a local football club or gymnasium or even a referee colleague employed in physical training, he is well advised to take personal advantage of such services.

Many officials are not so fortunate. What advice can be offered to them to improve physical capability? The referee is not required, as the players are, to develop the ability to jump to head a ball powerfully or to kick it. But he is required to accelerate quickly from a standing start, to have speed of movement and ability to manoeuvre over heavy grounds, to turn and change direction while in motion and to possess sufficient reserves of stamina to last more than two hours (allowing for matches where extra time may be necessary). To determine what improvements to his health may be required, the referee will know by analysing each game how efficient he has been in keeping up with the play, in moving to the positions selected after reading situations and what degree of fatigue he has experienced during the later stages of a hard game.

Basically then, what he needs to concentrate on are acceleration, speed, ability to manoeuvre and stamina. Most officials will have little difficulty in finding somewhere to run - a local sports track, park, heath, wood or road - in order to develop all four requirements. In very bad weather, for those who live in blocks of flats the stairways can be ideal alternatives.

It is advisable to adopt a personal physical routine to perform daily which includes deep breathing, bending and stretching exercises, press-ups, jogging, running and sprinting. The aim should be to progressively increase the level of performance until a satisfactory standard has been achieved. This may take several weeks, depending on the initial condition. Many officials play other sports which develop and maintain physical condition. Sports which demand co-ordination of observation, assessment of situations, speed of decision and physical action are particularly appropriate for the football referee. Such sports include tennis, squash, badminton, basketball, volleyball, handball, table-tennis, water polo and, of course, football itself.

When does an official know that a satisfactory standard has been reached? In several countries referee associations have devised training schedules and performance tests. In some a referee is not allowed to control matches until he has passed specified minimum tests. In a few the referees are tested more than once per season. The trend is towards more countries adopting minimum physical standards. Maybe in time all football-playing countries will insist that match officials reach a certain level of athletic performance before permission is granted to control organized matches. This is already the case with international referees, who are not accepted onto the FIFA list until proof has been presented that they have met the standards of the FIFA Cooper test. The introduction to the test and its minimum requirements are as follows:

Introduction
A modern football match can only be perfectly controlled if the referee is in a good state of health and has excellent reflexes. If this is not the case the referee runs the risk of not merely giving a bad performance, but also of endangering his health, both of which are most undesirable. An annual medical check-up and performance test are therefore essential, especially when one considers that referees are active from the age of twenty-five to fifty, at which latter age it is not uncommon for sudden deterioration in health and quality of performance to go unheeded.

It is therefore in the referees' own interests and in those of the National Association and of FIFA that the required controls be carried out. Moreover it is of paramount importance that referees work continually at keeping fit so as to avoid an abrupt deterioration in their condition.

A simple and effective control which can be carried out regularly between examinations and which is easily exercised anywhere is the Cooper Test.

The conditions laid down have been carefully worked out with close co-operaion of the Referees' Committee and the Medical Committee of FIFA.

Minimum requirements

Cooper Test The number of metres run over level ground for the duration of 12 minutes (style of running optional)
Minimums: 25–39 years   2,300 metres   40–50 years   2,000 metres

Basic values of Cooper

Age	18-29	30-39	40-49	50-59
Very poor	-1,750	-1,500	-1,250	-1,000
Poor	1,760-2,240	1,510-1,990	1,260-1,740	1,010-1,490
In condition	2,250-2,750	2,000-2,500	1,750-2,250	1,500-2,000
Excellent	2,760-	2,510-	2,260-	2,010-

Other minimums: 400m-run (track), 75 seconds; 50m-run (track), 8 seconds; shuttle run 4 x 10m, 11.5 seconds.

$$\text{Normal weight (kg)} = \frac{\text{height (cm) x average chest measurement (cm)}}{240}$$

The chest measurement is calculated by measuring over the mamillas and is the arithmetical average between maximum inhalation and exhalation.

Excellent mobility should be the aim of every referee. Having achieved it he must learn to use it intelligently, as the following example illustrates.

A Football League referee owed much of his success to excellent mobility. By being promptly on the scene he was able to exercise keen control. However, it was noted that on occasions he would use his acceleration and speed when it was not necessary. He was sometimes too far ahead of play. When the ball was unexpectedly intercepted, or a bad pass was made, he was caught out of position and had to cover the same ground again to reach the required viewpoint. When made aware of this fault the referee improved his performances considerably by more thoughtful use of his high standard of mobility.

Summary

Every game of football is a play performed just once and without a script. What the twenty-two performers will do is a mystery. Each has his own part in the play and appears from time to time but the director, the referee is required to control the action for every second. The enjoyment of the players (and of the audience, if there is one) depends a great deal on the success or failure of the referee to stay out of the scene until his direction is needed. He must have the ability to read situations accurately and to give intelligent direction quickly so that the story can continue to interest.

How the referee achieves reading ability has been the subject of this chapter. It is presented as a framework within which an individual can develop his own ability to read the predetermined factors and to make the best use of knowledge, experience and psychology with good mobility. Apart from helping the official to read the game, close study of some of the subjects, particularly the playing skills, will bring new interest and pleasure into his task. Attention to physical and mental preparation will not only improve his ability to control football matches. It will also develop personality and confidence in meeting the problems of daily life.

In chapter 4 the key to practical match control is given as *position*. Having now considered the importance of reading the game we see that the process which every referee has to follow is: *read – position – observe – decide – act*.

⑨ Gamesmanship or Cheating?

'Gamesmanship:
The art of winning without actually cheating'
(Stephen Potter)

'Gamesmanship' has become a common word in the world of sport. Stephen Potter, invented and defined it, and it has a certain ring of mischievous fun. It has become a popular term for small acts carried out in the course of a sporting contest intended to put an opponent off his stroke or gain an unfair advantage. Stress is placed on 'small acts' because, to keep within the humorous limits of the word, they should not appear too serious, should not disconcert the opponent too much, should not gain too unfair an advantage.

A slight noise, a cough or the rustle of paper, just as an opponent is about to attempt a skilful manoeuvre, say in a game of billiards or golf, may be enough to force him into an error. To qualify as 'gamesmanship' the action must appear to be accidental so that the intention behind it can be disguised. Although the opponent may suspect, he can never be really sure that the distraction was intentional, particularly if the distracter apologizes for disturbing his concentration. The damage has, of course, been done. The shot is missed and the incident is then classified under another heading, as 'all part of the game'. This term implies an unavoidable and unlucky break such as the unexpected bounce of a ball off an uneven surface which causes a player to mistime a hit or a kick.

In football the action of an attacker retrieving the ball for his opponents to take a goal kick may be applauded because it appears to be a sporting gesture to save his opponents the trouble of fetching the ball. However, the attacker's real intention was to retain possession of the ball long enough to allow him to regain his position. Only he knows this as a fact; others can never be certain.

If the 'gamesmanship' acts are designed to be more intimidating, extended into a series to unfairly influence the whole play, calculated and rehearsed with wilful intention, the humorous and mischievous connotation of the word disappears. It must be replaced by a much more serious and distasteful word, 'cheating'. No sportsman will be too upset to be accused of gamesmanship, but to be accused of cheating is intolerable because any success he may have achieved by skill is immediately suspect. A certain professional golfer was observed to commit an act of cheating in a competition. He was accused but denied the charge. He was disqualified from the competition but that was not the end of the matter. The publicity of the incident ruined his career. His action had put a question mark against his previous record as an expert player.

There is no clear dividing line between 'gamesmanship' and 'cheating'. The common link is the intention to gain an unfair advantage. Endeavouring to gain an unfair advantage is clearly contrary to the spirit of the game. Because the referee's duty is to safeguard this spirit it follows that he needs to be aware of what acts of gamesmanship or cheating may appear in matches under his control, in the same way that he must be aware of physical crimes and of misconduct (discussed in chapter 3).

This chapter is intended to help match officials first by explaining the background to gamesmanship, second, by quoting specific examples observed in actual matches, and third, by suggesting how the individual referee can extend his knowledge of the subject. The word 'gamesmanship' will be used throughout this chapter because of its general usage in the game. But the alert reader will recognize some of the examples as determined attempts to cheat.

Background

Gamesmanship is not a new phenomenon in football. It can be said to have started in the 1890s when the players' right to appeal for decisions (chapter 2) was abolished. The referee was charged with the whole discipline and control of the game, with power to punish what he considered to be intentional fouls and to dismiss players.

By this time professional football was established and growing in popularity. Paid players, whose livelihood depended on results, began to demonstrate skill not only with the ball but also in preventing opponents from scoring by committing deliberate fouls or by stopping the ball with the hands. The latter was directly responsible for the introduction of the penalty kick. These and similar acts became known as 'professional fouls'. Relationships between players and referee became cooler. The referee, an amateur, became the man to outwit. Because he represented authority, an undetected foul or an action which gained an unfair advantage was considered as a victory against authority and 'fair game'. The same attitude applies today and is called 'gamesmanship'. The only difference today is that the acts of gamesmanship are more numerous and sophisticated in character.

It is not so long ago that an England team manager shocked an audience of referees by declaring, 'I have to teach my players to be five moves ahead of the referee'. Maybe he was exaggerating to make his point, but the message was unmistakable.

The term 'professional foul', introduced when the professional game began to flourish, was probably meant to imply that such an action would only be committed by a low-paid professional in order to keep his job. At that time the true sporting game was amateur football and it may not have been of much concern that a few professionals, out of the one thousand or so employed in the 1890s, should commit such ill-mannered and ungentlemanly acts. In one sense the situation has not changed in that 'professional fouls' are committed by a small percentage of the total population of professional players. What has changed alarmingly, however, is the effect of these actions on football as a whole and on referees' task in particular, simply because of the change in the medium of communication.

Specific acts of gamesmanship, cheating or professional fouls – whatever label one wishes give them – can be observed in junior football and even in school games within twenty-four hours of being seen on television. Recently an eight-year-old boy returned home after playing for his school team and was heard to boast that he had committed 'a pro foul' on an opponent to stop a goal. His justification was that he had seen his idol, a professional of a Football League First Division team, do the same thing a week earlier. Many referees have reported examples of dissent by schoolboy footballers which, a few years ago, were unheard of. One referee reported having to dismiss his own son for swearing during a friendly match.

Gamesmanship, then, started when football became competitive. Considerations of employment and money rewards, prestige and glory, achievement of social positions beyond normal expectancy, have all been factors contributing to the growth of what has been described as 'the cancer of football'. The exciting skills of talented players have too often been blunted, submerged or even eliminated, by wilfully constructed practices born of an intensive study of the most minute influences on the results of matches. The basic principles of equality to demonstrate skill within the reasonable bounds of safety and to provide the maximum enjoyment for those who take part or watch are of no concern to those who contrive to win at all costs and to suit their personal ambitions.

It is sometimes said that top-level football will always be played with gamesmanship because the rewards of success are so dazzling. This was proved false by the manner in which the world's best players completed the 1970 and 1974 World Cup Final tournaments in Mexico and the Federal Republic of Germany, respectively. There can be no higher acclaim for an individual than world acknowledgement of his skill and sportsmanship. That such sportsmanship and entertainment was possible was due to the determination of FIFA to present football at its best, with rigid control, and to the co-operation of the team officials and players. If such results can be achieved at the highest level, they can, with similar determination and co-operation, be achieved throughout the game.

The referee will always be in the front line of the battle of wits to contain gamesmanship. The following guide to some of the specific actions observed in many matches should help him in his task.

Examples of gamesmanship

The following examples serve to demonstrate the range of gamesmanship acts which have been experienced and which may appear in future matches in the same form or with slight variations. All have the common denominator of abusing the spirit of the game.

DEAD-BALL SITUATIONS

1   *Place kick*

A minor but irritating practice is frequently observed where an attacker places himself in the opponents' half, sometimes with only one foot. Often the ball is then passed to this player who moves it back to a supporting colleague. Apart from not conforming to the law, the intention sometimes appears to be to test the reaction of the referee. Some referees consider the point to be too trivial to take action and miss an opportunity to demonstrate (a) that the action has been noted and (b) that the match will be controlled firmly from the first kick.

2   *Goal kick*

The goal kick is sometimes used as an opportunity to waste time either by the attacking or by the defending team.

a) A goalkeeper who wishes to waste time will move slowly to retrieve the ball from behind the goal-line, taking the longest way around the goal, pretending to test the hardness of the ball and bouncing it several times. After placing the ball he moves back behind his goal-line for a long run and takes more time signalling to colleagues to move into position.

b) In a similar time-wasting situation, the goalkeeper deliberately places the ball on the incorrect side of the goal area or just outside the area, knowing that seconds will be taken up while the referee or linesman corrects him. He may also pretend that he misunderstands instructions.

c) The ball is passed to a colleague who steps into the penalty area to play it knowing that the goal kick must be retaken.

d) After going through all the motions of taking the kick the goalkeeper calls on a colleague, usually outside the penalty area, to take it.

e) Attackers waste time by moving slowly out of the penalty area hoping to delay the signal.

f) An attacker retrieves the ball from behind the goal-line and then walks to a position outside the penalty area before returning the ball.

3   *Corner kick*

a) An attacker stands in front of the goalkeeper to block the view of the ball and restrict movement. The goalkeeper complains to the referee and asks for protection from the attacker when the ball is kicked, hoping to gain a free kick for the attacker's slightest movement.

b) A tall attacker places himself in front of a small linesman to obstruct his view of rehearsed foul play in the goal area.

4   *Penalty kick*

a) After the ball is placed the goalkeeper walks to it and tests it for hardness, bounces and replaces it. He has put the ball in a position different from that preferred by the kicker who then has to decide whether to put it in its original position or kick it as it lies. The intention is to disturb the kicker's concentration.

b) The goalkeeper protests that the ball is not on the penalty mark, to delay and to affect the kicker's concentration.

c) A defender walks in front of the kicker while the referee positions the players or is distracted by another defender. The first defender makes much of pointing to one side of the goal indicating to the goalkeeper that the ball will be kicked in that direction. If the kicker has chosen the same side he may decide to change the direction, with the possibility of missing the goal. If he has decided on the other side of the goal he may think that the obvious signal really means the opposite. Whichever way he thinks he could be in enough doubt to miss the goal.

d) When the signal is given a defender runs into the penalty area to be alongside the kicker as the ball is kicked. He knows that referees rarely caution for encroachment but, even if caution results, he may have disturbed the kicker enough to miss the goal. When the kick is retaken the goalkeeper now knows which is the favoured side of goal and has a better chance to save.

e) The kicker runs to the ball, stops, passes his foot just over the ball and then kicks it into goal after the goalkeeper has moved.

f) After a signal the kicker walks to the ball and bends down as if to change its position, but as his hands are about to touch it he kicks the ball hoping that the goalkeeper is unprepared.

g) A colleague of the kicker stands outside the penalty area behind and almost in line with the kicker. As the kicker runs to the ball the colleague makes distracting movements within the vision of the goalkeeper.

5 *Throw-in*

Gaining distance and wasting time at throw-ins appears in various forms.

a) The thrower obtains the ball, looks at his colleagues, takes a step or two back bouncing the ball, advances to the line but arrives two metres nearer to his opponents' goal-line. He then looks around again, signals to colleagues, bounces the ball and moves sideways along the touchline in the pretence of throwing. When the ball is eventually put into play several metres have been gained. When the throw-in is near to the opposing penalty area the advantage gained can be considerable if a long-throw tactic is employed.

b) To waste time a player will go through the usual preparations and when apparently ready to put the ball into play he will drop it and call a colleague to take over. Some teams will try this with three or even four players if the referee is weak.

c) In some time-wasting situations the thrower will attempt the action of 5a and when corrected will make much of asking for the location of the exact spot – a form of dissent intended to ridicule officials and gain sympathy from spectators.

d)   The ball is retrieved by a player for an opponent's throw-in. He walks to take up position before returning the ball (figure 72), or he offers the ball to the opponent and deliberately drops it before the opponent can take it, or he throws the ball to the referee many yards from the point of throw-in.

Figure 72   Delay at a throw-in

6   *Free kicks*

Free kicks awarded to the attacking team just outside the penalty area produce many incidents of the defence gaining time to obtain the best chance to negate the award. The serious view taken of these practices is discussed in chapter 2, Law 13.

a)   The ball is kicked by a defending player away from the position of the free kick (see figure 21), or is kicked or thrown to the referee, or is thrown to a colleague who throws to another until time is gained to move into position.

b)   A defending player stands close to the ball to direct a defensive wall from the goalkeeper's signals. His position is either in front of or behind the ball, but invariably within ten yards (see figure 89, page 178).

c)   If an obstructing player is cautioned another player is delegated to adopt the same tactics at the next free kick. (NB See chapter 7, free kicks, 'the wall': If the referee is of the opinion that a team is adopting the tactic described in 6c he is advised to inform the captain that any repetition may result in the dismissal of the offender whether or not he has been previously cautioned. This advice was the subject of a Notice to Referees of 29 September 1958 issued by the FA.)

d) A defender behind the ball and on his way to take up a position times his arrival at the ball just as it is about to be kicked.

e) An attacker places himself in the 'wall' with the intention of falling or moving away to leave a gap for the ball to be kicked through. The defenders counter by standing on the opponent's foot, pushing, kicking, using a knee to force him to move so that the gap can be closed.

f) An attacker links his arm through that of a defender at the end of the 'wall'. Just before the ball is kicked he moves back dragging the end of the wall to expose the goal.

g) When the ball is kicked a defender, usually at the end of the wall and nearest to the ball, is delegated to rush towards the kicker to 'take him out of the game', that is, to block any attempt to kick the ball from a reverse pass (figure 73).

Figure 73   Encroaching at a free kick

h) Attackers attempt to counter the defensive wall by moving the ball to one side when the signal is about to be given, to obtain a new angle of attack on the goal.

DYNAMIC PLAY SITUATIONS

7 *Intimidation*

Intimidation involves actions planned as a running campaign against an individual such as a key player, perhaps a clever distributor of the ball or a skilful player known to have a quick temper. Opponents try to intimidate him into committing an offence of foul play or misconduct so that he is cautioned or dismissed or appears to be the instigator of bad feeling among opponents.

a) *Off-ball situations*

An opponent may use verbal intimidation with threats of violence, foul or abusive language. Or when unobserved by match officials he may spit at the player.

b) *On-ball situations*

A calculated foul in the opening minutes, when referees do not usually penalize severely, may be enough to tempt the fouled player to retaliation.

c) *By goalkeepers*

To discourage attackers from challenges a goalkeeper may raise one foot in an intimidatory manner when catching the ball (figure 74).

Figure 74

d) *Irritating physical contact*

With hand, arm or elbow; grabbing the player's shirt on the blind side of officials; over-exuberant play; treading on a player's feet, legs or other parts of the body when the player has fallen; 'accidental' stumbling into the player, and other intimidating acts which fray tempers and stifle skill.

e) *Tackle from behind*

A feature of European football in the 1960s and 70s has been the increasing intimidation of opponents by fierce tackles from behind. From legitimate challenges for the ball with outstretched leg has developed closer body contact from the challenging player. This has increased to the extent where the tackled player is sometimes thrown forward by the impact of a collision with an opponent who appears intent on running straight through him (see figure 75). The practice has become so well established that training methods have been devised to build up the physique of both attacking and defending players to withstand the violence of these tackles. The player on the receiving end has no chance to control the ball and turn. Consequently, much skilful play is lost.

Figure 75

Referees have been urged to stamp out the vicious tackle from behind by taking firm action. The degree of punishment will vary according to the degree of intention assessed by the referee at each incident. A caution may be necessary or, in situations where the challenging player shows a total disregard for his opponent by crashing into his back, dismissal for serious foul play would be justified.

8   *False claims*

Frequently players appeal for throw-ins, goal kicks and corner kicks with the knowledge that their claims are false, hoping to trick the referee or linesman into giving the decision in favour of their team.

9   *False fouls*

Some players attempt to persuade officials that they have been fouled by falling spectacularly at the slightest physical contact. Similarly, others have been observed to fall dramatically without being touched. In other situations, often within the opponents' penalty area, a player will propel himself away from an opponent as if pushed.

10   *False injuries*

A player will commit a foul and then give the impression that he is injured, to gain sympathy or a less severe punishment.

11   *'Coached' injuries*

For no apparent reason a player will fall and pretend to be hurt so that the game is stopped. He has received a prearranged signal from his coach at a moment in the game when the opposing team are playing well. The intention is to take the opponents 'off the boil', to spoil their rhythm and concentration. The same act of 'gamesmanship' can occur several times in the same match.

12   *Coaching*

The intention of a player appearing hurt may be to stop the game so that coaching instructions can be conveyed via the person sent into the field to 'examine' the 'injured' player. In an international match a second player skilfully prevented the referee from listening in on the instructions by placing himself between the referee and the 'injured' player.

13   *Goalkeepers' reference marks*

A fairly recent trend in gamesmanship is for goalkeepers to use an artificial aid to positioning by adding marks to the field, for example, at the centre of the goal-area line. Some goalkeepers have been observed to make a mark extending eighteen yards from the centre of the goal to the middle of the penalty-area line. Others continue the six-yard lines to the penalty-area boundary and so on

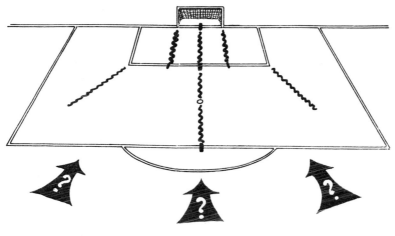

Figure 76

(figure 76). One was even observed to place white tapes on the places where he needed a reference point.

The practice has become so prevalent that some fields of play have been specially marked by the groundsman at the centre of the goal-area line to reduce damage to the surface from goalkeepers' boots. Such markings are illegal and referees are required to caution players (it is not necessarily the goalkeeper who adds these marks) observed carrying out this form of gamesmanship. It is sometimes argued that goalkeepers should be allowed reference marks if required. The counter argument is that it would be more appropriate to add markings to help attacking players to find the way to the goal, as in figure 76.

14 *Familiarity*

A subtle form of gamesmanship is attempted by the player who compliments the referee when decisions are given. Even decisions against his team are praised, but these are nearly always too obvious to be disputed. The referee may be misled into considering the player to be very fair-minded. That is the intention – the same player will later loudly claim a penalty when he or a colleague has fallen after physical contact with an opponent. A susceptible official may find it difficult to refuse the claim.

L

15   *Tactical fouls on the referee*

Just as key players may be subject to calculated gamesmanship, the referee may occasionally be taken out of the game at a vital moment by a player who 'accidentally' bumps into him. It is a ploy to distract the referee from another gamesmanship action, to divert him from his patrol away from the scene of specific gamesmanship tactics, to unsettle him so that he becomes confused and more easily influenced by unjust calls. A referee who finds himself apparently getting in the way of players should consider whether this form of gamesmanship is being employed before criticizing the diagonal system.

"Oh, dear — oh, dear — oh, dear — we are awfully sorry, ref"

16   *Deliberate handball*

There is a feeling of sympathy for the defender who saves a certain goal by deliberately stopping or catching the ball with his hands. The action is justified by the argument that the resulting penalty kick may fail. If a goal is scored then the defender has lost nothing by his valiant rearguard action. The International Board takes a more serious view and has instructed referees, in a memorandum of June 1957 and again in September 1969, that the practice must be dealt with by issuing a caution to the offender. This disciplinary action is not limited to the clear goal-scoring chance. Destroying skilful moves of opponents by catching or handling the ball may also justify the caution (see figure 77).

Figure 77   Deliberate handball

Extending knowledge of gamesmanship

In the course of his career a referee may officiate in a thousand matches and experience, say, fifty different acts of gamesmanship. One hundred referees will each experience a similar number. Of the total of five thousand probably ninety per cent will be common experiences such as those described in the previous section. This means that five hundred different acts are known by individual referees.

It would be ideal to be able to pool the experiences of the hundred officials so that every individual could be aware of the five hundred in addition to his own fifty. With such total awareness acts of gamesmanship would be immediately recognized and, with determined action, 'the cancer of football' could be cut out. Such an ideal can never be achieved, but at least the knowledge of this aspect of football can be more widely spread throughout the match-control side of the game. Here are four suggestions towards this aim:

1   *Personal observation*
Special attention to the study of the reading factors discussed in chapter 8, for

example, those concerning knowledge of play and of skills, will extend the official's personal dossier of situations where acts of gamesmanship are likely to occur.

2   *Group meetings*

At meetings of match officials in a local referees' association or at conferences of officials serving a particular competition, an illuminating subject for discussion can be particular match incidents experienced or observed since the previous meeting. Individuals should be encouraged to describe personal experiences and the group discussion which follows often leads to valuable contributions from others.

3   *Coaching dossier*

Coaches of match officials should consider maintaining a dossier of gamesmanship acts for the instruction of new officials, and expand the dossier from the results of such group meetings as those mentioned above.

4   *Practical demonstrations*

Where it is possible to assemble groups of referees on a marked field of play a useful practical session can be arranged as follows:
a)   The group is divided into sub-groups of six to ten referees.
b)   Specific situations are allocated to each sub-group, for example, throw-in (1), corner kick (2), penalty kick (3), free kick (4), goalkeeping (5).
c)   A sub-group leader is appointed to control the session and to report to the chief coach.

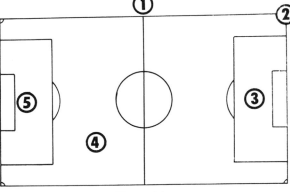

Figure 78

d) Each sub-group then moves to its allocated position (figure 78), and discusses as many gamesmanship ploys, within the time available and the experience of its members, as apply to its specific situation.

e) The sub-group leader records all experiences.

f) Each sub-group agrees on three items and rehearses a demonstration.

g) All sub-groups are brought together and each demonstrates the three chosen items, moving to the appropriate areas of the field for realism.

h) After all demonstrations are completed questions are discussed and advice given on methods of dealing with specific problems.

i) A report listing all incidents of gamesmanship issued to the participants will serve as a personal dossier for future extension.

As well as pooling knowledge, this type of group session is an entertaining means of developing confidence among those who are normally silent at more formal meetings.

Summary

The object of this chapter has been to lay bare an aspect of the game which has existed for nearly a century. Its effect on the pleasures of football has become so widespread, through modern methods of communication, that it can now be seen at all levels, from international to schoolboy football. Every referee will experience incidents usually described as 'gamesmanship' or 'professional fouls' which are no less than determined attempts to cheat. Appeals to team managers, coaches and players to control these incidents have not produced a noticeable change of attitude, for the need to win has grown more urgent as rewards have become more glittering.

To describe gamesmanship as 'the cancer of football' is not overstating the point when the exciting skills of talented players are denied to the game by calculated and ruthless tactics. The referee is in effect the surgeon appointed to cut out the cancerous growth, but unless he is trained to know what to look for and where to find it his task is impossible. The growth will continue to suffocate sporting play.

The greater use of linesmen in detecting and reporting gamesmanship has to be considered. Players are less likely to attempt gamesmanship if the referee indicates his awareness of the subject by dealing firmly with the first incidents. The referee can never be one move ahead of the players but with more exposure to the topic the chances of being five moves behind will become smaller.

10 Playing Tactics and the Referee

Should the referee be concerned with the tactics of play? The referee who officiates in junior football may feel that he is unlikely to be concerned, but it is a fact that tactics figure in some form at all levels, from the 'kick-and-rush' of enthusiastic schoolboys who follow the ball as a swarm of bees follows its queen, to the highly sophisticated almost computerized systems of tactics employed at international level. At the first level the tactics are dictated by the movement of the ball. At the highest level they are calculated in advance of the first kick.

At junior level a team may not plan tactical play, but listening at any match will reveal that a great deal of tactical advice is given in the calls of players to colleagues. Most of this advice may fall on deaf ears, but calls such as 'drop back', 'move forward', 'mark their outside-right', 'hold the ball', 'pass it to me', 'pass it back to the keeper', can be heard from the youngest of players. They have the same idea in mind as players in an international match, that of making the most of the situation, of improving team performance, of affecting the course of play.

We have seen in chapter 8 that one of the predetermined factors in reading a game is the attitude of players, and that attitudes are conditioned by various influences including coaching instructions and team tactics. This chapter stresses the connection between playing tactics and the referee. It draws together some of the important aspects of practical match control (chapter 7), reading a game (chapter 8) and acts of gamesmanship (chapter 9) in the form of tactical fouls. A few tactical fouls are described and suggestions given on extending your knowledge of tactical play.

1 The connection

Why is it necessary for referees to become aware of the tactics employed during a match? The short answer is – for better control. Better control will come from the application of tactical knowledge in assessing situations, in predicting more accurately the next phase of play, and in deciding more quickly what action is required.

By the call in a junior match to 'mark their outside-right', the referee should be alerted to the possibility of closer physical contact between the marking player and the opposing outside-right. In most cases the call may lead to nothing more than a few fair tackles from the defender. On the other hand, if the defender is an aggressive player, a whole series of fouls may be attempted. Having heard the call and realized its possible effect the referee will be ready to deal quickly with the first sign of unfair play.

At higher levels the need for all three match officials – the referee and his linesmen – to understand tactics becomes more vital and the task more complex. Team managers and coaches are highly critical of the number of referees who appear unable to read the deliberate campaigns of tactical fouls directed against key players in tactical plans. The problem is serious enough to affect team selection. As well as his ability to weigh up the opposition and the tactics likely to be employed, the efficiency of the referee to detect off-the-ball fouls must be taken into account. If there is little confidence in this respect in the nominated official, a sensitive and talented forward player may not be risked against an opponent well known for his provocative spoiling tactics.

The effectiveness of an aggressive defender of this type was observed recently in the final of a European national cup competition. An internationally known player, acknowledged for his individual flair in tactical positioning and in creating openings in front of goal, was harassed, intimidated and provoked by the same opponent throughout the match in a series of undetected fouls off-the-ball. He finished the match thoroughly dejected nursing many bruises. An illustration of one of the many fouls he had to suffer is shown in figure 79. In the face of such treatment his composure was remarkable. It appeared to confirm the statement from a respected coach that he needed to devote much attention to the conditioning of similarly gifted players to accept verbal insults, manhandling, spitting and other vile acts from opponents delegated to stifle their skills. This is also an appalling indictment of the failure of very experienced referees to detect such practices when close man-to-man marking tactics are employed. In the past it has been enough for referees simply to know the laws and their general interpretation. It has become increasingly evident in recent years that the referee engaged at higher levels must understand more about the game and what is being attempted tactically.

Figure 79   'Dealing with the key opponent.'

Following the 1970 World Cup tournament in Mexico a report of the FIFA Technical Study Group stated that, '... the training of referees should be carried out as assiduously as the teams taking part in the competition. Referees must keep up with the constant development of the game.' A similar but more pointed comment appeared in the report on match control prepared after the 1974 series in the Federal Republic of Germany: 'Somewhere there seems to be a gap between the "old rules" and the modern game. The refereeing somehow has not been able to keep pace with the tactical progress in play.'

In chapter 7 it was concluded that position was the key to efficient control at dead-ball situations. A better understanding of the tactical formations of players and what is likely to be attempted when the ball is put into play must add a refining touch to the judgement of position. In chapter 9 and at the beginning of this chapter we have noted acts of gamesmanship that have a tactical aim – withdrawing the ball, time-wasting, stifling skill, physical intimidation, changing the course of play, giving coaching instructions. A better understanding of what influence tactical planning has on these incidents must be a positive factor in reading the situation, moving to the best position and making the correct decision. These are the factors which connect playing tactics and the referee.

2   Playing tactics

Authoritative works on team systems and tactical play are available for officials who want to study the subject in depth. In this section a few observations are made to draw the reader's attention to some aspects of tactical play which may be more readily discernible, and serve as an introduction to what the referee needs to know as he progresses through various levels of the game.

a)   *Styles of play*

Different styles of play present different refereeing problems. The style adopted by a team will depend on the level of skill and intelligence of the players, the skill of the managers and coaches, and national or local psychological characteristics. Qualified observers have described the British style of play as extremely fast, frantic at times, with emphasis on dominating mid-field play and relying on power in tackling for possession. South American styles appear to rely on possession play in making slow-building attacks using close interpassing movements. In Germany in 1974 Holland introduced what is now described as 'total football', involving fluidity of movement, mass attacks on the opposing goal, and sudden rushes upfield when the ball is cleared from defence to leave opponents stranded in off-side positions.

These may be oversimplifications but they should serve to illustrate differences in styles which will pose different problems of match control. With the style of play which relies on close marking and quick, determined tackles the referee will be required to interpret many problems of physical contact. With a more open style, involving long passes and quick running, the referee will be concerned that his mobility is adequate to judge positional situations such as off-side. Becoming efficient at recognizing styles of play is sound preparation for reading the changing tactical situations in a game.

b)   *Possession*

Whichever team is in possession of the ball is able to dictate the tactics. The next move could be the first of many which puts the ball into the opposing goal. Therefore a team in possession is said to be attacking even though the ball may be inside its own penalty area. Its effect on players is to switch their tactics from defensive to offensive, to take up different positions to make use of the advantage of possession. Opponents have then to think defensively, adjust their forces to meet the threat and attempt to regain the ball.

A team in the lead may be content to retain possession with interpassing movements backwards or square. This tactic will require an assessment of positioning by the opposing players (and by the referee) different from that which applies when the attacking team are intent on getting the ball to the opposing goal area as quickly as possible. In figure 80 the player with the ball will be assessing:

1   positions and movements of colleagues
2   positions and movements of opponents
3   what angles are open for passes
4   the types of pass he needs to make, that is, long or short, hard or soft, low or high, etc.
5   whether to hold the ball to draw an opponent and create space for a pass to a colleague
6   whether to retain the ball and move
7   directions open to him to retain and move.

An opponent facing the player in possession will assess:
1   whether to make an immediate challenge for the ball to reduce the time factor
2   how to reduce the angle of passing, that is, the space factor
3   the likely direction of a pass to another opponent
4   whether to force the possessing player into a less dangerous area
5   the position of supporting colleagues if a direct challenge should fail.

Other players of the team in possession will be moving to:
1   receive a pass
2   cover the player with the ball in the event of his losing it in an imminent tackle
3   draw opponents into unfavourable positions with decoy runs
4   leave space for another player to run into to receive the ball.

Other players of the defending team will also be moving to reduce the time and the space available, funnelling back towards their own goal, closing gaps, setting up screens of seven or eight defenders, or moving upfield to leave opponents in off-side positions.

The decisions of the player with the ball, his challenger, his colleagues and of other opposing players will determine the next phase of play. Therefore the better the referee's assessment of the next move the better are his chances of anticipating potential infringements. The beginning of tactical play, then, is possession. Each time the ball is lost or given away the tactical situation is reversed. Wherever the referee is at that moment he must reassess the tactical possibilities for his next positional decision.

Figure 80   In possession

c)   *Marking tactics*

The two types of marking tactics are 1) man-for-man marking, and 2) zone- or space-marking. The former involves close proximity between defender and attacker (figure 81) in order to put the player with the ball under pressure, forcing him into errors of timing and judgement. This tactic is fair providing that the defending player uses fair means to challenge for the ball. Where several defending players are marking tightly it is often more important to observe what is happening off the ball. Intelligently coached attackers will be moving, as mentioned previously, to open up more space. A defender who has been outwitted may indulge in holding or tripping tactics to thwart the good tactical play of his opponent. Also, the attacking player may attempt to gain a second or two on the defender by pushing him off balance as he starts his run.

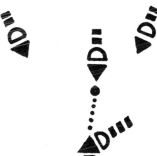

Figure 81   Man-for-man marking

Zone- or space-marking is more concerned with protecting spaces which could be dangerous if attackers became able to place the ball in them so that colleagues could threaten the goal or open up other avenues to goal. In other words, the attack is directed at a space instead of at a player. Defenders are allocated zones to patrol and they pick up attackers who move into these zones. Figure 82 illustrates the system adopted by a leading Football League First Division team. Attacker 7 has entered the zone patrolled by defender 3, who moves out to challenge. Defenders 6, 5 and 2 are ready to protect their zones by moving to challenge a square pass, A, or a high ball to the goal area, B or to cover across if 3 is beaten by the attacker, C. On many occasions a combination of man-for-man and zone-marking will appear; the former as the attacker enters the danger area, that is the last third of the field, the latter as the ball is played into the opposing half. Intelligent reading of marking tactics will alert the referee to the options open to the player in possession.

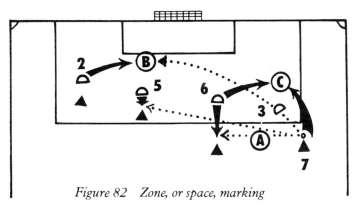

Figure 82   Zone, or space, marking

d)   Passing tactics

Teams favouring long passes to forward positions can pose problems of mobility for referees. Close off-side decisions can also result from attacking players accelerating quickly past opponents. Some teams rely on short passing movements for progress towards the goal. Alternatively, close marking by opponents may impose these tactics.

The 'wall pass' is a common tactic to gain space and time, to commit defenders into hurried tackles. The player acting as the wall will often receive contact from behind (figure 83). Sometimes the tackle is too severe and needs immediate action.

Figure 83   Wall pass

Alternatively, the wall pass can leave the initiating player in a good position to run at goal and a problem of advantage will need solving. Variations in long and short passing may be the feature of some teams. The ball will be contained in defence with a series of short passes until an opening is seen for a quick forward pass (figure 84). Keeping an eye open for gaps appearing ahead of the ball should be of as much interest to the referee as it is to the team in possession.

Figure 84   Short–long passing movement

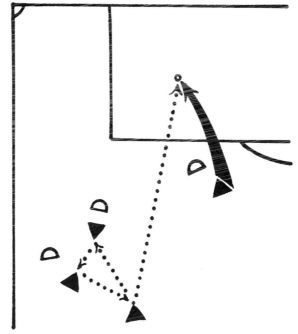

One aspect of long passes applies to possession by the goalkeeper. A feature of the tactic of one Football League First Division club is to combine the ability of its goalkeeper to kick the ball long distances with the exceptional acceleration of a forward player (figure 85). This tactic, which switches defence to attack in a second, has produced vital goals against teams unprepared for the move. It has also caught several referees and linesmen out of the position required to judge accurately off-side situations and offences committed against the forward after he has passed his marking defender. The cause is often a problem of 'ball-watching'.

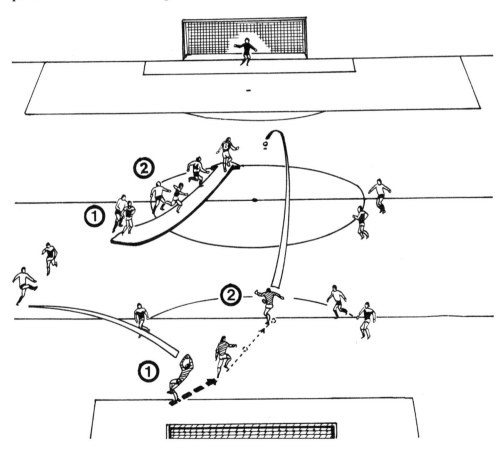

Figure 85   Attacking from possession by goalkeeper

In figure 85 the goalkeeper obtains possession from a shot at goal, 1. This is the moment for the forward to check the path to goal and to begin his turn past his opponent. The goalkeeper has made the most of the penalty area by rolling the ball to the boundary line. When he kicks it, 2, the forward is in an on-side position and accelerating fast. When he receives the ball he appears to be off-side and has sometimes been unjustly penalized. An excellent tactical move has been frustrated. The forward has been subjected to holding, shirt-pulling, obstruction, ankle-tapping and other impeding acts when he started his run past the defender while the ball was in the air. In addition, the same player has been guilty of initiating foul play by handing off his opponent to gain time and distance. This example reinforces the advice given in chapter 8 to study the skills of individual players.

Reverse passing tactics can surprise match officials as well as opponents. An attack may be mounted with short passing movements across the field towards a corner (figure 86). The point of attack is then switched suddenly by a reverse pass to a supporting player who moves the ball quickly across to the other side of the field directly to a colleague or into a space for him to run in and obtain possession or shoot for goal.

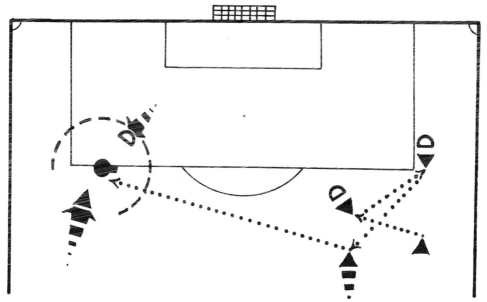

Figure 86   Reverse passing: danger zone for referee

This is a particularly important point for referees who find themselves interfering with play. In following the direction of play for the first phase of the attack, the referee should be alert to a reverse-pass situation so that he is clear of the subsequent cross-field movement of the ball. Several referees have been observed to spoil a sound tactical move by lack of awareness of what is being attempted. The most dangerous place for this problem is around the corner of the penalty area as shown. To avoid interference the referee may have to consider taking a path towards the touchline that takes him behind the receiving player. Moving backwards can be too slow to be effective and can obstruct a supporting attacker. Moving forwards can confuse and obstruct defending and attacking players. It will almost certainly involve hundred and eighty degree or even three hundred and sixty degree snap turns to avoid players and ball. During these vital seconds control is lost because the official is concentrating on avoiding action instead of on potential foul play or off-side situations. Sometimes the best move for the referee is to stand still!

Interpassing movements by a team in the lead may be intended to slow down the pace of play, to draw opponents forward into abnormal positions leaving gaps behind which can be exploited by a quick counter-attack. It has been observed that opposing players become frustrated when the ball is successfully withheld for what seems to be a long time. Challenges and tackles become more uncontrolled. If the referee is slow to appreciate the effect of such tactics he will not have positioned himself in the best place to deal promptly with foul play, retaliation and violence.

e)   *Off-the-ball tactics*

The observation made earlier in this chapter that officials should be aware of what is happening away from the ball is worth more detailed study.

Running off the ball is not always intended to put the running player in a good position to receive it. An individual or a group of players will attempt to open up possibilities for a colleague. In figure 87 a simple tactic is illustrated showing *8* and *10* moving in opposite directions to open a gap for the ball to be fed forward to *9*. Similar movements are designed to stretch the defence towards the touchlines, to leave more space in the front of the goal for an advancing colleague in possession. This tactic is a counter to defensive concentration on retreat in front of and within the penalty area. Overlapping and blind-side runs, common in tactical play, have the similar objectives of drawing opponents out of position, increasing the number of possibilities for

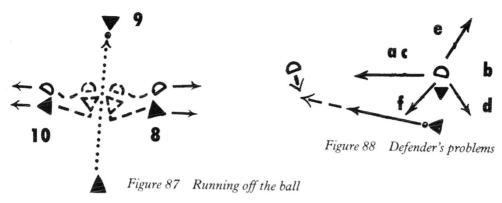

Figure 88   *Defender's problems*

Figure 87   *Running off the ball*

passing or shooting, or obtaining a numerical advantage.

Off-the ball tactics pose constant problems for defending players. Should the marking defender (figure 88) (*a*) move with his opponent, (*b*) stay to cover space, (*c*) pass on his opponent to another colleague, (*d*) attempt to achieve an off-side situation, (*e*) move back towards goal or (*f*) advance for a direct challenge on the player in possession? How the problems are solved depends on the defender's ability to read the purpose of the move and to find a satisfactory countermove. At times the easiest solution may be to commit an offence on the immediate opponent in the hope that it will not be detected because it is away from the area of concentration around the ball.

f)   *Dead-ball tactics*

At dead-ball situations the attacking team have the initiative to create goal-scoring tactics. It is recognized that about forty per cent of all goals are scored as a direct or indirect result of free kicks in or near the penalty area, from corner kicks and throw-ins. The attacking team have undisputed possession of the ball and the opportunity to put it into play while opposing players are forced to withdraw ten yards – a situation which rarely appears in dynamic play. It becomes clear why defensive tactics will be based on introducing delay so that the defence can be organized before the ball is put into play. This is understandable, but not acceptable. We have already discussed the purpose of Law 13 in chapter 2 and stressed the point of reducing delay and eliminating obstruction. In chapter 7 the dead-ball situations have been examined to determine good positions. Aspects of gamesmanship in some of these situations have been highlighted in the previous chapter.

M

What kind of tactics is the referee likely to see at dead-ball situations? From the attacking side, there might be (a) a quick kick which often means allowing the ball to be put into play before opponents have retreated ten yards, or (b) devised tactics at a 'set piece' situation where delay is inevitable and opponents have won time to organize. There is also the possibility that the attacking team *want* the defence to build a wall so that several opponents are committed to a particular and predictable space. The opportunity then arises for more players of the attacking team to be advanced, thus gaining a numerical advantage in spaces away from the wall.

In setting up a wall the defence will attempt to seal off the goal partially or completely from a direct shot. The number of players in the wall will be determined by the angle of attack of the goal and whether the kick is direct or indirect.

Figure 89

Figure 89 shows a typical defensive formation facing a direct free kick from a central position in front of goal. The end of the wall is directed in line with one post by another defending player standing behind the ball and working in conjunction with signals from the goalkeeper. The goalkeeper covers the unprotected side of goal.

At free kicks from positions near the edge of the penalty area the formation of the wall is likely to be as shown in figure 90. Apart from blocking the shot at

Figure 90

goal, defenders are likely to be stationed at each end of the wall to attack the ball or an opponent as soon as the ball is played, particularly from an indirect free kick (figure 73). To surprise and confuse are often part of the tactics of the attacking team. When two or more attackers are close to the ball, the chances are that a decoy tactic will be used. One player may run to the ball, followed by a second or even a third, to set the defence a problem of when to move and to disguise the direction of the kick. Before taking up his position the referee may have been involved in moving defenders back and in dealing with potential trouble between players of both teams unwilling to give ground. A quick assessment of the disposition of the players away from the immediate vicinity of the ball should alert the referee with some knowledge of tactics to the likely movements of attackers and counter-moves of defenders. He can then decide his best viewing position, but may be required to find an alternative if he is likely to interfere with the ball or with the players. This last point recalls the comments made on reverse passing movements. On many occasions referees have been seen to become mixed up in the play immediately following a free kick because they have not assessed the tactical situation and/or taken up a position clear of play before giving the signal.

When free kicks are awarded in mid-field or in the defending third, some teams adopt the tactic of putting the ball into play quickly to catch opponents out of position. Not only should the referee encourage the tactic, but he should have read it in time to be on the move to his next vantage point. He should at least be one move ahead of the opposing players because only he knows that a free kick is about to be awarded.

g)   *Corner-kick tactics*

No two corner kicks are identical. One awarded in the opening minutes of a match can be quite different from another awarded near its end. At some there will be as few as six players in the penalty area. At others, as many as twenty. Including the kicker twenty-one players can be involved in tactical play at a corner kick. From some corner kicks the ball will be played short to a supporting colleague to draw defenders towards the ball and to obtain a more direct angle of approach to goal. Defenders sometimes counter his move by moving away from the goal-line to set up off-side situations. More often than not the ball is kicked directly towards the penalty area with inswinging or outswinging spin. Because of the danger of this type of kick much attention is given by well-coached teams to moves and counter-moves.

Figure 91

Figure 91 illustrates a few typical tactics observed in the higher levels of football. The tactics are described below and some comments are included on the type of incidents which can occur before the ball arrives into its target area.

1 To gain the maximum space between the ball and the corner post for an inswinging kick, the ball is placed at the extremity of the quadrant where it meets the goal-line.

2 To limit the flight path of the ball and the accuracy of the kick, a defender will be delegated to take up a position as close as possible to the ball. The effect of this tactic is illustrated in figure 92.

Figure 92   Limiting the 'flight path'

3 An attacker positions himself on the side of goal nearest to the corner kick either to deflect a short dropping ball backwards into the goal area or to divert it to a supporting colleague at 7. He can be the target of pushing or shirt-holding by a defender.

4 An attacker positions himself immediately in front of the goalkeeper and moves back into his opponent or across his path when the ball is kicked. Defenders suspecting this action may push, hold or kick the attacker.

5 Three attackers are positioned to make a 'pressure run' towards a high ball placed to arrive at head height near the penalty mark in the hope that one will head it into goal. A tightly marking defence will be alert to this move and tactical fouls may occur by deliberate obstruction, holding, pushing, charging or tripping. Attackers also use a tactical foul here by pushing in order to obtain a clear path to the ball.

6   A decoy run by an attacker across the goal, intended to draw a defender out of position and create space for a colleague, is often stopped by deliberate obstruction or shirt-pulling.

7   An attacker stationed at 7 to divert a hard, low corner kick into goal or to receive the ball from 3 is sometimes the target of obstruction or pushing.

Of these few examples only 1 and 2 can be controlled before the corner kick is taken. The others can occur in a confusing mixture of offences, some by attackers, some by defenders, within the space of a few seconds. However, the referee has the advantage of delaying the signal for a moment while he makes an assessment of the disposition of players, tactics likely to be attempted and potential trouble spots. Referees who give some time to the study of corner-kick tactics will rarely find themselves positioned in exactly the same place twice.

h)   *Throw-in tactics*

At some levels of the game the throw-in is considered simply as a method of putting the ball back into play. At high level the throw-in is an important opportunity to employ tactics which can be as rewarding as free kicks near goal or corner kicks because, apart from other reasons, both defending players and match officials tend to lose concentration. An intelligently coached team will be aware of this fact and use it to their advantage by taking the throw-in quickly before defenders have taken up man-for-man marking or are covering vital spaces.

For the referee and nearest linesman it is important to recognize the intention behind the quick throw and to be prepared to apply advantage by not being too pedantic about the position of the throw-in. To stop play and have the throw-in taken from the exact place where the ball crossed the touchline could destroy a vital goal chance. Similarly, the referee should exercise caution when a player appears to be wasting time at a throw-in. For example, in figure 93 the thrower delays his throw because his colleagues are tightly marked. At a given signal from the thrower they accelerate past their opponents and the ball is thrown ahead into a space behind the defenders. If the referee has lost his patience with the thrower and blows the whistle for him to hurry just as the ball is delivered, it may be necessary to have the throw retaken. This will not only take up more time but will disclose to the opposing defenders a carefully rehearsed tactical move.

Figure 93   *Delayed throw-in*

Long throw-in tactics can be profitable sources of goals. In figure 94 the defence appears to have covered all attackers by tight marking. The thrower may have the ability to throw the ball high to the far post (particularly on a narrow field of play) for heading chances. Or he may use a tactic to open up space which involves delivering the ball to the feet of a colleague who has advanced towards the thrower at *A*, drawing an opponent away from goal. He then starts a run along the touchline, taking his marking opponent, but checks back quickly to receive a return pass in a clear space at *B*. The point of the attack is then switched quickly by placing the ball into one of the spaces created by colleagues who have also drawn their marking opponents away from goal and are now running towards these spaces, *C* and *D*.

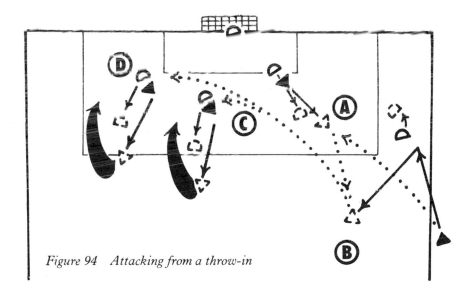

Figure 94   *Attacking from a throw-in*

Figure 94 illustrates a combination of tactics such as man-for-man marking, a reverse pass, a long pass into space and movements off the ball, drawing opponents away from spaces intended as targets in the next phase of the attack. For the referee this poses two immediate problems, (a) how to position in order to avoid interfering with off-the-ball movements and (b) possible off-side situations when the ball is kicked towards areas *C* and *D*. Skilfully executed tactics similar to this example are a pleasure to watch. The apparently aimless lob towards the penalty area takes on a new meaning. The referee who appreciates what is being attempted will be reading the moves of the players more intelligently and will be prepared for illegal counter-measures by defences caught out of position.

i)   *Tactical fouls*

A tactical foul is intended to take an opponent out of the game by deliberate foul play when he is attempting to take up a strategic position. In figure 95 an attack is developing on the right at *A*. Linesman *L1* is moving along the touchline looking for possible infringements between attacker *7* and defender

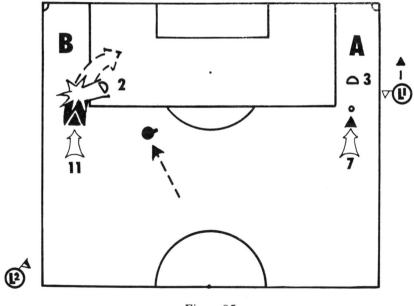

Figure 95

3. He is also occupied in watching the ball when close to the touchline, potential off-side situations and in retaining his balance if he is moving backwards. The referee *R* is moving left on his diagonal, watching for infringements between *7* and *3* and for signals from his linesman. On the referee's blind (left) side, at *B* attacker *11*, anticipating a cross-ball from the right, starts on a run behind defender *2*. The move is seen by *2* who runs into *11* and knocks him to the ground. With *11* temporarily out of the game *2* becomes an uncommitted defender, thereby gaining what is probably a decisive advantage for the defence in destroying a goal-scoring opportunity.

To detect incidents of this type the referee needs to glance away from the immediate area of play to survey potential tactical foul situations. Linesman *L2* has an important role in this respect, as discussed in chapter 5.

j)   *Tactics and conditions*

Predetermined factors discussed in chapter 8, such as size of playing area, surface condition, wind, sun and other variable elements, will affect playing tactics. The abilities of players to pass the ball, judge its flight and bounce, turn quickly, accelerate, jump, tackle and shoot will be restricted or assisted accordingly.

The size of the playing area alone could drastically change the tactical play. For example, tight man-for-man marking and covering of space will be more difficult on a large playing area than on a small area. Free-kick tactics near goal can be designed to use space on a large area or short passing moves on a small area. On a small area there are greater opportunities for exploiting throw-in and corner-kick tactics. Also the role of the goalkeeper becomes more important in setting up attacking moves. In this respect forwards will be given the defensive task of restricting the opportunities of goalkeepers to deliver the ball accurately to colleagues near the halfway line. The use of the long goal kick is likely to be favoured, whereas on a large area the short kick to a defender, a return pass and a kick-out-of-hand by the goalkeeper may be more effective.

The position and strength of the sun may be used by a team to direct long, high passes so that opponents have difficulty in judging direction and pace.

k)   *Substitutes, injuries and state of play*

Tactics can change dramatically at a substitution, an injury to a key player or a sudden swing of fortune in the state of play.

A tall substitute may be introduced to change tactical play from short, low crosses from the touchlines to high centres, taking advantage of a weakness observed in the heading ability of a central defender. A key player, handicapped by injury, may have to be moved to another position or be provided with extra cover.

The state of play can have a marked effect on tactics. A team with a leading margin of one goal may try to contain play and introduce delaying and time-wasting tactics. The opponents are likely to take risks by throwing more players forward, particularly at free kicks and corner kicks. In this situation, which is likely to appear towards the end of a match, the referee must be accurate in his assessment of tactics. One mistake on his part could result in failure to observe an incident which has a decisive effect on the whole match.

"Before we toss, there's something you ought to know-we've got a slope problem"

Extending knowledge of playing tactics

Most of the observations in this chapter may appear to apply only to the highest levels of football, but it would be unwise for match officials at junior and intermediate levels to make this assumption. Tactical coaching is becoming more widespread as more people become qualified coaches and as coaching aids improve. Officials in junior football will observe tactics copied from professional teams seen in action live or on the television screen. It is probable that these will be relatively simple tactics and appear mainly at dead-ball situations. But they will be tried and should be known.

The referee at higher levels should consider the impact of coaching on the pattern of play in the second half of every match. The first half may have been relatively easy to control, but at half-time tactical instructions can put a completely different complexion on the second period. If it is assumed that the second half will be the same as the first the referee and his linesmen could be in for a shock in the opening minutes after the restart. Whatever the referee has read into playing tactics in the first half should be reappraised from the moment he signals the start of the second. At this level the referee is advised to treat each match as two separate matches of forty-five minutes.

To extend your knowledge of playing tactics it is helpful, although not essential, to attend courses for coaches on the theory of coaching. Alternatively or additionally, close contact with individual professional coaches or a coaching association will provide opportunities for the discussion of tactical play. If the reader is a member of a referees' society he can try to persuade society administrators to invite leading coaches to give lectures and demonstrations at regular meetings or at referee courses.

Studying tactics when viewing matches live or on film or television is excellent preparation. Note basic formations and the function of certain players. Identify the key players with special skills for winning the ball, accurate distribution, excellent control in possession; the key attacker to whom the ball is frequently directed to make use of his flair for beating opponents. Having achieved some measure of success in reading these factors note the simple tactics employed at dead-ball situations. Throw-ins, corner kicks and free kicks near the penalty area are particularly important and fruitful sources for tactical play information.

Assess the general style of play of a team, for example, whether reliance is placed on physical power or on technical skills. Note the change of formations when the ball is given away or lost to the opposing team. Put yourself in the position of the player with the ball and assess options available for passing, dribbling, shooting, etc. and assess the manner in which the player solves the problem of what to do next. Study the movements of attackers and defenders in the immediate playing area. After some practice in weighing up tactics close to the ball, extend your vision to observe what others are doing further away. Listen to the tactical calls and gauge the effect of action which may follow.

What type of marking tactics are employed? Does a team favour long or short passing movements? What influence has the goalkeeper on initiating attacks? In particular watch off-the-ball tactics. Having identified a key player, concentrate on what he is doing and what tactics are employed by opponents to counter his influence on play. Note tactical foul situations and methods used to stop opponents moving into position. Judge the influence of the size of the playing area, its surface condition and the weather on tactics throughout the match. What effect on play results from injuries, substitutions or a change in score? There need never be a dull moment in any match observed by match officials who are keen to extend their knowledge of playing tactics.

Summary

This chapter has stressed the connection between playing tactics and the referee. To be knowledgeable in the laws of the game is only the beginning of intelligent match control. It is necessary for referees to be knowledgeable in the positive and negative aspects of tactical play so that a constructive tactic is not unwittingly frustrated or a destructive tactic overlooked. The game of football has in recent years become sophisticated in many ways, and perhaps most of all in tactical development. The scoring of a goal is not always the result of planned tactics, however. Many goals are scored because of simple errors in defence, a deficiency in skill by a particular player, a bad pass, a mistimed tackle. Teams cannot rely on mistakes to win matches but playing tactics can, and often do, force opponents into error by reducing time and space. The more sophisticated the tactics become the less time and space are available. The message for match officials is the same. For effective control, tactics must be assessed more quickly.

Apart from knowledge, the other reading factors discussed in chapter 8 such as physical and mental capabilities need constant sharpening to keep the referee abreast of fast-flowing tactical play at top levels of the game. 'Total football' demands 'total refereeing', that is, control of all phases of play over the whole field.

11 Refereeing Around The World

by Ken Aston

Chief FIFA Lecturer for Referees' courses

It would be generally true to say that judges, umpires and referees in any sport have started off with some experience as participators. The greater the experience, the more likely a person is to become a competent official. This is certainly true in football, and in those countries where the playing of the game developed rapidly to a good standard it was found that further progress was limited by a low standard of refereeing. Many who were persuaded to take up the whistle found that their experience of the game itself was insufficient. A good example of this was in South America, when in the early fifties it was found necessary to raise the standard of refereeing in order that the playing standards could continue to rise. A number of British referees were contracted to referee in the more progressive South American countries, and through their example and instruction standards eventually rose sufficiently for the presence of British referees to be no longer necessary.

What was true of South America has been repeated many times over in countries where football at a high competitive level is comparatively new: the standard of refereeing has lagged behind the standard of play. When Sir Stanley Rous (an ex-international referee himself) became President of FIFA in 1961, he began to extend his coaching scheme worldwide. He had developed this first-class scheme in England during his years as Secretary of the FA, and his coaching included referees. Thus it was that lecturers from FIFA began to travel the world - sometimes spending two weeks in one place with referees concentrated there for a course, and sometimes undertaking an extensive tour staying at each place perhaps only two days. It was always very demanding on the lecturer's stamina, ingenuity and ability to make the best of the facilities provided; in many places these were minimal and sometimes almost primitive. However, in the last fifteen years the standards have slowly but very surely risen, and there are clear signs that the general improvement is gathering pace.

The performance of referees from all continents in the final series of the

World Cup must, of course, be the ultimate criterion of world standards. It is not too many years ago that the Referees' Committee of FIFA had few reliable countries outside Europe from which to select their referees for this showpiece series. In 1974 they were able to use referees from countries such as Senegal, Egypt, Australia, Canada and Singapore, who refereed their matches in Germany with considerable efficiency. This is the direct result of the FIFA programme of education.

When one considers the wide spectrum of races, climates, temperaments and languages from which all players and referees are drawn, it is inevitable that some differences must arise in the playing of a body-contact game. Brought up in the football background of one particular country, referees too tend to interpret the laws as generally accepted by the players in that country. Clear differences existed between South America and Europe; European players objected to shirt-pulling and obstruction, while South Americans objected to over-vigorous tackles and especially the tackle from behind. Most of these differences have been resolved, and the laws are interpreted and applied by referees much more uniformly than ever before. Complete uniformity – even within one country – will never be entirely achieved, simply because all men have different degrees of courage in any given set of circumstances. Two principal factors have been responsible for the great improvements in interpretation by referees and their acceptance by the players: first, the efforts of FIFA by means of courses, memoranda, films and other means of communication and second, the 'briefing' conferences of the World Cup referees immediately preceding the final series.

In Santiago, Chile, in 1962 the referees met briefly before the finals started, received their appointments, were given a few administrative details and some encouraging remarks, and from then on it was a case of *sauve qui peut*. This applied not only to the matches and their attendant problems but also to the referees' spare time, of which there was a great deal. Referees got to know few of their fellows, and none belonging to the other language groups. There was no exchange of views and no spirit of teamwork, and on the whole morale was low. The first real effort to take advantage of this gathering of top referees was made when the World Cup came to London in 1966. A very full hospitality and entertainment programme was arranged for the thirty referees, the aim being that they should form themselves into a corporate body as well as enjoy their stay in England. As a result, morale was high and teamwork improved. Short daily conferences were arranged each morning after matches, and common problems were discussed as well as varying interpretations. These conferences were so much better than nothing, but even they had only limited success. It was often a case of 'locking the stable door after the horse had bolted', and at any one time more than half the referees were at other sub-seats and were not able to take part.

The major breakthrough came in 1970 in Mexico. The World Cup in England had been marred by unpleasant incidents, and several star players including Pelé had been put out of the game by injury from unfair tackles. The South Americans, especially, complained about the refereeing of the matches, at times with some justification. It was for these reasons that the media forecast that the 1970 World Cup in Mexico might never finish. The pessimistic sports writers and commentators painted a backcloth of violence and temperaments as hot as the Mexican sun under which the matches were to be played. Also, the matches were to be played at an altitude of seven thousand feet, and all participants (including referees) would have to arrive at least two weeks before the competition for altitude acclimatization. Here, then, was a ready-made opportunity to have a pre-competition conference of real significance and to lay the foundations of a well-disciplined World Cup.

The thirty referees were divided into the four official language groups – English, French, German, and Spanish. A large conference room with simultaneous interpreting facilities was arranged, and each referee attended each session for ten days. A film had been made showing sixty incidents from top class matches, including World Cup matches from the previous series and other international matches. The incidents had been selected with particular reference to the grey areas of interpretation, and to actions in the game which should not be tolerated by referees. The film also set out to reinforce and illustrate a memorandum from the Referees' Committee of FIFA, issued in 1969, which defined the fairness and unfairness of certain types of tackle – especially the tackle from behind. It dealt also with other practical problems in the game, as will be seen at the end of this chapter. The film was shown on the first day without the sound commentary. It was pointed out that these incidents were real and not simulated, and that they were likely to occur in the ensuing World Cup matches. Each of the four language groups then discussed each section of the film day by day. They demonstrated their views practically to each other on the training field, and then came back to the conference in the afternoon with a group decision. The conference discussed each view and then came to a common decision. Sometimes it was necessary for a little give and take, but all agreed to implement to the full all decisions taken. It must now be revealed that a calculated risk had been taken by the Referees' Committee of FIFA. The film had not only been made with a commentary which it was both hoped and expected that the conference of World Cup referees would agree to implement, but copies had been made with the commentary in other languages for distribution to all competing nations! In the event, the commentary was exactly in accord with all conference decisions – as was demonstrated on the last afternoon when the film was shown to the referees with the sound switched on.

All this, however, was only part of the way towards ensuring well-disciplined games. On too many occasions decisions are taken by groups in authority without the people most concerned being informed – they learn of the decisions from hard experience. In football the co-operation of coaches and players is absolutely vital if the games are to be trouble-free. So the next step was to issue a memorandum clearly laying down the decisions and interpretations arrived at the conference, together with a copy of the film already mentioned. After studying and digesting the memorandum and film, the coaches and Heads of Delegation were invited to ask questions to clarify any points not quite clear. This done, it was then necessary for press, television, and radio commentators to be informed, and so the memorandum was issued in the various languages to the press centre. It might have seemed that nothing now remained to be done. Not so. It had to be shown that the words meant what they said and that the referees would back up their words by deeds. This was ably demonstrated by Kurt Tschenscher of West Germany in the opening match between Mexico and the USSR: five players were cautioned and everyone realized that the referees meant what they said. In the remaining matches not one player was sent off and it was agreed by everyone that this was the best disciplined World Cup so far. Of course, it was not perfect and there were clear areas for improvement in 1974.

In the opening game in Mexico City the five cautions had been administered for the first time in a new way – by the card system. This system originated at a bad-tempered match in the World Cup in 1966 between England and Argentina, refereed by Rudy Kreitlein, a West German who spoke only German. It had always been a problem to caution a player if you didn't speak his language. You blew the whistle rather strongly, recorded the number on his back, and then made it as clear as you could by the expression of your face and suitable gestures that if he offended again he would be sent off. The morning after the Argentina match the Charlton brothers read in the morning press that each of them had been cautioned by the referee, though each claimed to be unaware of this at the time. The card system was therefore thought up to overcome the particular problem of language in international matches. Since its great success in Mexico in 1970 the use of the cards has spread universally and into domestic competitions, for it has other advantages. The showing of the yellow card seems to quieten other players as well as the offender himself and leaves spectators and commentators in no doubt as to what action the referee has taken. Referees, however, must take care that they do not use the cards too readily just because it is an easy thing to do.

Certainly the standards set in Mexico were good for the game in the following years, and it was hoped that the 1974 World Cup in West Germany would at least maintain the discipline and behaviour shown in 1970. This would depend on the quality of the referees selected and the goodwill and cooperation of the players. FIFA were determined that standards would be raised even higher, and set about the all-important task of selecting the referees. This in itself is difficult. It is the prime duty of FIFA to promote and develop football in all countries of the world, and at the beginning of this chapter it was pointed out that playing standards can be held back by poor refereeing. One of the ways of improving refereeing is by encouragement, by letting all referees know that the top honours in the game are open to them if they are good enough. A referee from a country not well known for its achievements in football who officiates in the final series of the World Cup is able on returning home to share his experience and new knowledge with his colleagues. They in turn see that they also have a chance of distinction if they dedicate themselves.

It was for these reasons that two referees were appointed from Africa, Asia, and CONCACAF (representing the Caribbean and America). The Referees' Committee of FIFA drew up a list of eighty likely referees at their meeting in Buenos Aires in February 1973, and special attention was paid to these officials by observers. In Cairo in September 1973 this list was reduced to fifty when the reports received had been studied. The final thirty were selected at a meeting in London in February 1974, and it was agreed that a similar conference to that held in Mexico was imperative, though it need not be so long, since there was no altitude problem.

The conference in fact lasted for just over a week, during which time the most thorough medical and physical checks were carried out on the referees by

N

a specialist team of German doctors, and a rigorous training schedule adhered to. The method used in the conference was much the same as in Mexico, based on a film made from the matches played at the last World Cup in that country. It was agreed that in addition to the problems dealt with in Mexico special attention would be paid to time-wasting, dissent from decisions, exceeding four steps by the goalkeeper, and treatment of injuries on the field of play. Many comments were made after the series about how successful the referees were in eradicating these incidents from the matches. Once again the memorandum written after the conference (which was based on the Mexico document) was circulated to all teams and the media, and again the film illustrating the points was shown to all coaches at a meeting where questions were asked and answers given.

One particular matter dealt with at the conference did not appear in the memorandum. This was the question of linesmen. The standard of lining at previous World Cups, including Mexico, was lower than it should be. International referees may not have acted as linesmen for some years when they find themselves appointed linesmen in a World Cup match. Further, they have to work with a referee who is virtually a stranger to them – indeed, it is very likely that they do not speak the same language, though every effort is made to facilitate communication between the three officials in the dressing-room before the match. Some time was therefore devoted to the technique of lining, rather in the nature of a refresher course. A clear improvement in the standard of lining resulted, but it still did not reach the very high standard demanded by such important matches. Serious thought will have to be given to the appointment of a team of three officials from the same country, two of them active and very experienced linesmen, for the final series of future World Cups. After all, this is what is done in the qualifying rounds!

The referee's job continues to get more difficult as the pressures increase. In some countries there is pressure not only from players and clubs who are determined to win at all costs and from the press and television, but from representatives of the national government. Many referees belong to their country's government youth and sports department and as such come under the direct control of a government official. It is not difficult to see how in such a situation politics can bring its influence to bear on a man who wishes to be as impartial as possible.

The FIFA/Coca-Cola project has been designed for the development of football in all countries where help is needed, and teams consisting of lecturers in administration, medicine, coaching and refereeing have already made many visits. With these continuing efforts one looks with confidence towards ever-rising standards. The countries who so far have had the lion's share of refereeing honours may one day find their share is a good deal smaller.

Précis of referees' conferences and resolutions affecting team managers and players

FIFA WORLD CUP 1974

The following matters were discussed and all the referees agreed unanimously. All decisions are in accordance with the laws of the game. This précis is issued only as a guide to team coaches and may not be quoted as an authority; the decision in many cases is a matter of the referee's opinion, and this opinion is formed only at the time of the incident. Team coaches are requested to bring the matters listed to the attention of their players.

Tackling
1   With foot lifted from ground. This is permissible unless it is *seen* to be dangerous to the opponent.
2   With both feet together. Also permissible unless *seen* to be too dangerous to the opponent
3   Sliding tackle, with one or both legs. This is permissible but if the ball is not played and the opponent is tripped, the punishment will be a direct free kick.
4   Tackle from behind. If the ball is played without the first player touching his opponent's legs, this is allowed. If a player is tripped by an opponent attempting to play the ball from behind, a direct free kick will be awarded. Charging from behind is not allowed unless the opponent is *intentionally* obstructing.

Offences against goalkeepers
The following will be penalized:
1   Standing in front of him at corner kicks etc. without trying to play the ball.
2   Jumping at him under the pretence of heading the ball.
3   Raising the foot as the goalkeeper kicks the ball from his hands.
4   Standing in front of him to obstruct him when he is trying to clear the ball.

Four-step rule
An indirect free kick will be awarded against a goalkeeper who exceeds the permitted four steps. All goalkeepers must be reminded that, though the law has been broken frequently in the past, in the future it will be more strictly applied by referees.

Illegal use of arm

Many players use their arm to hold off an opponent. This is an offence under Law 12 and will be penalized by a direct free kick.

Scissors or bicycle kick

Permissible unless there are opponents near and the kick is dangerous to them.

Jumping at an opponent

A player who jumps at his opponent as if to head the ball in order to prevent his opponent from heading it will be penalized by a direct free kick.

Obstruction

Running across an opponent's path to retard his progress is unfair obstruction. Players who obstruct when the ball is not within their playing distance (that is, they cannot play it even if they wish to) will be punished by an indirect free kick.

Free kicks

1   Indirect free kicks will be signalled by the referee raising his arm; he will not raise two fingers as is the practice in some countries.
2   Players who in any way delay the taking of a free kick by their opponents will be cautioned (yellow card). On repetition, they will be sent from the field (red card).
3   Players who rush forward from the 'wall' before the ball is kicked will be cautioned the first time. The second time, a caution will again be given if a different player is involved.

Substitution

The substitute must bring the completed official card to the reserve linesman at the halfway line. The number of the player to be substituted will be clearly displayed on a board and this player shall immediately leave the field. The substitute may enter the field when permitted to do so by the reserve linesman, who acts on behalf of the referee.

Coaches and trainers

1   No coaching from the side of the field will be allowed. Only two team officials may enter the field when called by the referee.
2   Injured players must be treated *off the field of play*. If necessary, they will be removed by stretcher.
3   Since the two team officials will be permitted to enter the field only to *assess* an injury but not to treat it, and if necessary to arrange the removal of the player, it

would seem that only a minimum of medical materials should be carried to the field of play.

Substitute players and coaches

The five substitutes and five team officials must place themselves away from the field of play in the seats provided.

Attitude towards referees

Protests against the referee's decision will result in a caution. Any player who molests the referee will be sent off without caution. The *captain* of the team has no special rights but is responsible for the conduct of his team.

Players catching the ball

Players who catch the ball to prevent an attack developing will be cautioned.

Serious fouls

A player who commits a deliberate physical foul against his opponent will be dealt with severely by the referee; he may be sent from the field without previous caution.

Persistent infringement

Players who persistently infringe the laws of the game will be cautioned.

Throw-ins

Throw-ins will not be permitted to be taken from more than one metre from behind the touchline.

The 'lifted' free kick

The free kick 'lifted' with one foot will be permitted in this competition.

Time-wasting

1   Time-wasting by any player when the ball is out of play will not be permitted and the player concerned will be cautioned.

2   Time-wasting by the goalkeeper when the ball is in play will be dealt with under Law 12.5 (b).

Inspection of studs

The referee assisted by his linesmen, will inspect the players' studs as they go to the field in the corridor leading from the dressing-room to the field.

Team sheets

The team named first in the official list of matches will be called upon to complete the team sheet first.

12 Match Analysis and the Assessment of Referees

What was the standard of performance of the FIFA World Cup referees in 1974? What problems appeared? What further work is required to improve individual and collective performance?

In the previous chapter Ken Aston has given the inside story of the problems of coordinating the efforts of a multi-national group of officials in the 1966, 1970 and 1974 final competitions of the FIFA World Cup. Each final series provides a unique opportunity to study match control problems over a large number of matches during a short period. With the considerable aid of the mass media much detailed information is made available on the teams and their backgrounds, progress through to the final series, probable tactics, key players and their playing skills and many other factors contributing towards the skilful reading of a game as discussed in chapters 8, 9 and 10.

The pattern of match control throughout the world is established at these football showpieces. It is therefore important for referees to analyse the work of the international officials chosen to demonstrate the required standard. Few referees are able to travel to the country where the finals are played but most can follow the series by watching films or television broadcasts.

This chapter deals in the first section with observations noted during the 1974 series, together with others taken from the report of the FIFA Technical Study Group. In the second section official guides to the assessment of referees, from junior through to international level, are quoted so that each individual will have knowledge of what is expected of him.

1974 FIFA world cup: analysis of match control

Between 13 June and 7 July 1974, thirty-eight international matches were played in the final stages of the World Cup in the Federal Republic of Germany. They were controlled by thirty referees and four others appointed to act only as linesmen. Photographs of the officials and personal information appear in the appendix.

The policy adopted by the FIFA Referees' Committee was to allocate one match to each of a group of twenty-four officials for the opening matches, holding six of the most experienced in reserve for later rounds. The select six were joined by the six most successful referees of the first group. During the thirty-eight matches five players were dismissed and eighty-six cautions were issued. Seventy-one players were involved in these disciplinary measures. Only two games were completed without the need for the referee to produce either a yellow or a red card (these were Sweden *v.* Bulgaria and Brazil *v.* East Germany). One match resulted in one dismissal and four cautions. An incident in this match unseen by the referee was later dealt with and the offending player was suspended for three international matches. The incident had a most unfortunate outcome for one referee, as is explained later.

These are the statistics. What of the matches? The following are summaries of detailed personal notes taken during the games. (* marks points of particular interest.)

OPENING MATCHES

THE FIRST FINAL ROUND (TWENTY-FOUR MATCHES)

Sixteen teams competing in four groups, the first and second of each group qualifying for the second final round.

MATCH 1, BRAZIL V. YUGOSLAVIA, GROUP 2, 13 JUNE 1974, FRANKFURT

Referee	Rudolf Scheurer (Switzerland)
Linesman L1	Vital Loraux (Belgium)
Linesman L2	Luis Pestarino (Argentina)
Conditions:	dull, cool, rain, field soft, no wind
Diagonal:	left wing to left wing
Ball:	white, plain
Notes	1) Brazilian goalkeeper wears black stockings, rest are in white.
	2) Yugoslav goalkeeper wears black shorts, rest in white; also wears grey stockings, others red.

Minutes of Play *First half*	*Comment*
0.30	Tackle from behind by Y
3	Push by Y
4	Kick B
6	Push B
9	Two-footed tackle B
10	Obstruction Y
12	Charge from behind Y
13	Trip Y
15	*Field becoming muddy – sliding tackles for ball – fair
15.30	Push B
17.30	Tackle from behind B
18	*Caution – not retiring at free kick Y8
19	Trip Y
21	Push from behind Y
22	Dangerous tackle Y
23	Dangerous play B
24	Use of arm B
25	Trip B
25.20	B jumps into Y
26	*Referee using advantage well
29	Shirt pulled Y
29.30	*B appears to feign injury – R insists B taken off – remains off 2 min.
30	Push Y

Minutes of Play First half	Comment
31	Tackle from behind B
32	Y held in penalty area but is able to shoot
32.30	Trip B *Use of thigh by B when in possession, across opponent
38	Dangerous tackle B
38.30	Push B
38.40	Obstruction B
40	Handball Y *R on same side as L1 when kick taken
42	Obstruction Y
42.30	Trip Y
44	Tackle from behind B

28 free kicks

Second half	
	*Same diagonal
1	Dangerous tackle Y
3	Trip B
4	*B2 obstructs opponent while B1 obtains ball *Y10 cautioned – showing dissent at free kick
5	Tackle from behind B
5.30	Tackle from behind B
6	Push B
7	Dangerous play Y
8	Push Y
13	Charging at wrong time Y

Minutes of Play Second half	Comment
13.30	Obstruction Y
17	Obstruction Y
21	Push Y
23	Obstruction Y
26	Obstruction B
27	Push B *Wall 7-8 yards when kick taken
30	Trip Y
31	Violent charge B
34	Tackle from behind Y
37	Trip Y
40	Trip B
41	Trip Y
42	Handball B
43	Tackle from behind Y
44	Push B

24 free kicks
Result 0-0

Summary

1   2 cautions – encroaching and dissent
2   52 free kicks
3   No off-side
4   Pushing   11
    Tripping   10
    Tackles from behind   8
    Obstruction   8
    Dangerous play   7

Use of arm	1
Handball	2
Charging, violent	1
Charging from behind	1
Jumping at opponent	1
Shirt-pulling	1
Charge, wrong time	1

5 Use of hand and arm by both teams when in possession.

6 Use of thigh by B players – stepping across opponent when in possession – as extension of screening.

7 Goalkeepers' colours (shorts, stockings) differ from teams'.

8 Referee showed excellent control; used advantage well; dealt promptly with injured player.

This is a typical analysis indicating the pattern of offences which were spread fairly evenly throughout the match. A cautious opening match by both teams was probably the reason for no off-side offences.

MATCH 2, WEST GERMANY V. CHILE: a similar log was kept. Extracts are as follows:

Referee	Dogan Babacan (Turkey)
L1	Jack Taylor (England)
L2	Werner Winseman (Canada)

Minutes of play
First half   *Comment*

1   *Bad tackle from behind by C7; R – long talk to C7.

13   *C7 cautioned for tripping G when whistle blown for free kick.

44.30   Obstruction by C inside penalty area. End of half signalled before kick taken. Seemed unfair on G.

Second half
2   Deliberate handball by C. Mid-field cross pass but blatant. C cautioned.

4	Good advantage when G pulled back when in possession and in good scoring position.
8	At free kick C rushes to within three yards before ball kicked.
10	*R speaks with whistle – effective.
13	*Trip C2. Cautioned after R lets steam out of situation.
24	*C7 dismissed for kicking. R again waited for excitement to cool before producing red card. Some dissent by C players but not persistent.

Summary
1 23 fouls; 12 off-side
2 Excellent control by referee.
3 Excellent technique in dealing with explosive situations by achieving relative calm before indicating action.
4 Excellent whistle technique; signals calm, authoritative. Advantage decisions excellent. Wall control excellent with one exception (second half – eighth min.).
5 C7 dismissed in sixty-ninth min. after bad first min. foul and thirteenth min. caution.

This match provided referees with many excellent examples of positive control in a calm and efficient manner. In contrast a later match produced the following observations.

1 R weak – missed many off-the ball incidents against a particularly clever player.
2 Blatant over-the-top tackle resulted only in verbal warning in addition to free kick.

In the match Poland *v.* Argentina, excellently refereed by Clive Thomas (Wales), an interesting feature was the number of occasions the referee was seen to be interfering with play around the edge of the penalty area during the opening thirty minutes. Later he adopted a 'stand-still' policy which solved the problem. See chapter 10, passing tactics.

In another match the referee allowed too much intimidation, was weak in controlling defensive walls at free kicks (most were taken with opponents five or six yards away) and took no action at obvious gamesmanship tactics.

During the match between Italy and Argentina a player was deliberately obstructed – a free kick was awarded and both players offered to shake hands.

When Poland played Haïti a free kick was awarded outside the Haïti penalty area. The referee, 'George' Suppiah of Singapore, clearly indicated an indirect free kick. The ball was kicked direct into goal. When a goal kick was awarded the referee was accused of bias towards Haïti by a commentator who was obviously unaware of the laws of the game.

At the start of the much publicized match between East and West Germany the latter team's goalkeeper wore an all-black strip. At half time he changed to a green jersey. In the same match the other goalkeeper was cautioned for time-wasting and a player was shown the yellow card for receiving injury treatment on the field and refusing to be put on a stretcher. The foul count in this very important match was only twenty-two, well below average.

Holland *v.* Bulgaria was excellently controlled by Tony Boskovic (Australia) and produced the first penalty kicks (two) of the final series. One penalty kick was retaken because of encroachment by an attacking player. He was also cautioned. In a close-marking, quick tackling match, tackles from behind were a feature but were strictly actioned by the referee. Examples of blatant body-checking were observed which were interpreted as obstruction. Their effect on play, to stop quick-raiding opponents, deserved a direct free kick.

After nearly two thirds of the matches had been played, general summary notes included the following:

1   Standard of performance generally excellent – firm handling of physical offences and dissent, time-wasting, and treatment of injured players; substitution procedure smooth and efficient.

2   Linesmanship and teamwork between officials excellent, much improved on 1966 and 1970.

3   We have seen:
a) cautions for deliberate handball

   b) substitutes allowed to warm up along touchline in normal playing strip –
potentially confusing for linesmen judging off-side

   c) one referee using whistle signal to restart play at goal kicks

   d) two goalkeepers wearing gloves which appeared heavy and possibly
dangerous

   e) in all matches observed the referee ran the same diagonal, left wing to
left wing, in both halves

   f) generally excellent wall-control with one or two glaring exceptions

   g) some important off-the-ball incidents unobserved by the referee

   h) 'advantage' signal confused with 'play on, no offence': referee unjustly
criticized

   i) relatively few acts of gamesmanship

   j) many goalkeepers wearing shorts or stockings in colours different from
their teams; black preferred

4 We have not seen:

   a) impeding of goalkeepers either at corner kicks or when in possession

   b) abuse of possession by goalkeepers

   c) mass player protests or manhandling of officials

   d) coaching from the touchline

THE SECOND FINAL ROUND

During the second final round of twelve matches, several interesting match
control points were noted. Most were of a positive nature; a few indicated the
need for more coaching in technique, even at this level where only the most
experienced and the most successful officials from the first round were
employed. Among the observations noted were the following:

1 *Poland v. Yugoslavia*, referee Rudi Glockner (East Germany)
Penalty kick awarded to Poland for an off-the-ball kick at an opponent. An
excellent example of not watching the ball and awareness of tactical foul
play situations.

2 *West Germany v. Sweden*, referee Pavel Kazakov (USSR)

   a) Player cautioned for pulling back an opponent by grabbing his shorts.

   b) At penalty kick referee Kazakov controls encroachment *before* taking
position 1 (see chapter 7).

3   *West Germany v. Poland*, referee Erich Linemayer (Austria)
   a) Excellent use of advantage on almost flooded field.
   b) Quick action on tackles from behind.
   c) Clear hand signals assisted control.

4   *Brazil v. Poland* play-off for third and fourth places, referee Aurelio
   Angonese (Italy)
   Two incidents in this match, well controlled by referee Angonese, are of
   particular interest:
   a) The first occurred in the seventh-third minute when a Brazilian player
       in possession advanced on the Polish goal. An opponent grabbed him
       when outside the penalty area but he managed to retain possession and
       continue for about fifteen yards when he finally fell inside the penalty
       area. The referee had blown the whistle before the Brazilian fell and
       awarded a free kick outside the penalty area. The incident prompted the
       thought that a delayed signal may have resulted in a penalty kick despite
       the fact that the offence was initiated outside the penalty area. The
       offending player was justly cautioned.
   b) The second incident led to the only goal of the match which resulted in
       Poland taking third place. Lato, Poland, pushed the ball forward a few
       yards in the outside-right position when Kapka was standing in an
       off-side position in the centre. The linesman raised his flag to signal
       Kapka off-side but Lato ran forward to take control of the ball and
       referee Angonese waved play on. Lato ran on to score. This incident was
       almost identical to that which occurred in the match between West
       Bromwich Albion and Leeds United, discussed in chapter 4.

Among the points of negative match control noted in other matches were:

5   Several dangerous tackles were allowed in one match where the playing
   surface was very wet.

6   At a free kick near the penalty area the referee tried to physically push the
   defensive wall back when not more than six yards from the ball. He gave
   up when the players did not co-operate and signalled the kick to be taken.

7   A vital penalty kick was saved by the goalkeeper after he had clearly
   moved before the ball was kicked. The final score was 1-0 in favour of his
   team.

8   In another match the same goalkeeper again saved a penalty kick but had clearly moved first. Fortunately, the result was not affected. His team lost 0-1.

9   In a vital match, time lost through a long delay for attention to an injured player was not allowed.

10   The colour of ball boy's strip was almost identical to that of one team.

11   During the match Holland *v.* Brazil, an off-the-ball incident occurred which is recorded in the official FIFA report as having caused a change of mind in the choice of the referee to take charge of the World Cup Final. Bob Davidson (Scotland) had been chosen by a sub-committee to be recommended as the official in charge, but when the full committee met the incident had a decisive influence and Jack Taylor was appointed. The incident was that of a Brazilian Mario Marinho who, as film evidence later proved, butted an opponent, behind the referee's back. The opponent was knocked unconscious. Bob Davidson stated later that he did not see the offence. The committee clearly considered that it was his duty to see it. He paid a high price for this one oversight.

   The point of quoting this incident is to stress the vital role of linesmen in helping the referee to deal with incidents which occur off the ball or when he is unable for any reason to observe them himself. It is of interest to note that Holland, who introduced 'total football' to the FIFA World Cup, should be one of the teams in this match. The coincidence lends weight to the observation which concludes chapter 10 that 'total football' demands 'total refereeing' – even by linesmen! From others' misfortunes lessons can be learned. We will see in the following analysis how the match officials were able to profit from the misfortune of Bob Davidson.

The FIFA *World Cup Final 1974, West Germany v. Holland, 7 July 1974, Munich*

Referee	Jack Taylor (England)
L1	Ramon Barreto Ruiz (Uruguay)
L2	Alfonso G. Archundia (Mexico)

To be appointed to control the World Cup Final under the circumstances previously described could be expected to adversely affect the performance of the man given such enormous responsibility. In the case of Jack Taylor the challenge was accepted with the determination to prove that the choice was right by his thorough preparation and his strict control from the first whistle. In his pre-match briefing of the linesmen, Taylor faced a problem of communication. Neither linesman could speak or understand English sufficiently well to allow detailed discussion of match-control policy. However it was not too difficult to confirm the basic system of communication, that is, the use of the flag, running to the corner flag for corner kicks, running back to the halfway line for good goals or standing still if a problem arose. These matters had been well covered in the pre-tournament conference and in subsequent analyses of matches as the tournament progressed.

It was arranged that the linesmen would be particularly alert to events off the ball or behind the referee's back, to avoid a repetition of the Holland *v.* Brazil incident. How to communicate information of such incidents was the major point to be agreed on, for there could be no verbal consultation. Both linesmen were given the responsibility of judging any incident unseen by the referee as if they were in charge, and to decide what action should be taken, whether by caution or dismissal. The linesmen were well experienced international referees and could be entrusted with such responsibility.

The method of communicating was simple and effective. Small red and yellow cards were given to each linesman with the instruction to write on the appropriate card the number of the offending player and a letter, H or G, to signify his team. For example, if German player 4 committed an offence for which the punishment would be the issue of a caution, the linesman would be expected to write 4G on a yellow card. The card would be concealed in the linesman's hand so that only the referee would be aware of the intended message. The method worked well, as will be explained later.

On a warm, dry, sunny day the players and officials waited patiently for the colourful ceremonies of speeches and presentations and the playing of national anthems to come to an end before breaking away from the formal line-up to flex muscles and feel the turf. In front of a battery of cameramen and a capacity audience the toss-up was decided. Then occurred the first of several sensational events. Jack Taylor realized that the six flagposts marking the corners and halfway lines were missing! The start of the match was delayed while the posts were found and hurriedly put into position. They had been removed to avoid interfering with the opening pageantry. A second sensation occurred within sixty seconds of the whistle to start play. Holland were awarded a penalty kick before a German player had even touched the ball!

Johann Cruyff, who had proved to be one of the star players of the tournament, was tripped by Uli Hoeness as he advanced on the German goal. Neeskens converted to put Holland into the lead. The third sensation was a caution in the third minute to Vogts for kicking Cruyff.

The 'Cruyff penalty' in the 1974 FIFA World Cup final

In a matter of three minutes Jack Taylor had demonstrated that he had complete control of himself and the twenty-two players.

After twenty minutes a free kick was awarded to Holland. While the referee's back was turned, Van Hanagen of Holland pushed Müller to the ground. Players started to shout and protest as Taylor turned to see Müller prostrate. He could have no idea of how Müller got there or who was responsible – if indeed an offence had been committed. After calming down the players Taylor noted that linesman Archundia was raising his flag and moved over to consult him. Without exchanging words Taylor returned and produced the yellow card to caution Van Hanagen. He had seen a yellow card in Archundia's hand with the written message – 3H. The method had worked perfectly. The decision to caution the Dutch player was accepted without dissent and the game got under way.

Careful pre-match preparation and a good understanding between the officials prevented what could have been an ugly incident spoiling an otherwise absorbing tactical battle between two highly skilled teams. Five minutes later, another sensation – Overath was tripped inside the penalty area and Taylor immediately pointed to the penalty mark. The incident was not as clear-cut as the first but Taylor was in an excellent position to judge the intention of the challenge. Breitner scored from the penalty to equalize at 1-1.

Apart from these examples of positive match control, others were noted which are listed below to reinforce some of the points of practical refereeing covered in previous chapters.

1   Several players, of both teams, attempted to trick the referee into awarding free kicks by falling dramatically after physical contact with an opponent. Jack Taylor read these situations accurately. He made it clear by suitable gestures and hand signals that he was aware of what was being attempted and was not fooled.

2   Taylor also read the tactical situations well in recognizing the close attentions of Vogts on Cruyff in the opening minutes, which resulted in the caution for Vogts.

3   A consistently strict policy was followed in the first half which produced four cautions, one German and three Dutch players being shown the yellow card. It was not necessary to caution a player in the second half.

4   The last caution occurred as the players were leaving the field for halftime. Cruyff was seen to approach the referee and gesticulate in a manner which suggested dissent. He was waved away to the dressing-room but turned to continue his discussion with the referee who, by producing the yellow card for all to see, demonstrated that such conduct would not be tolerated.

5   After thirty-five minutes a lineman's off-side signal was overruled because the referee had seen that the ball was last touched by a defender.

6   Six minutes into the second half a serious incident was averted by prompt action when Cruyff committed an act of dangerous play on the German

goalkeeper, Maier. The referee clearly warned Cruyff to moderate his challenges on the goalkeeper.

7   Two foul throw-ins, the first seen in the tournament, occurred and were acted upon in the second half – more examples of consistent strict control.

8   Wall control at free kicks was faultless; similarly the application of advantage.

9   The match produced seven off-sides, two foul throw-ins and forty-one fouls of the following categories:

pushing	13
tripping	10
tackles from behind	5
obstruction	4
kicking	2
charging dangerously	2
handball	2
dangerous play	2
jumping at opponent	1

By the end of the 1974 FIFA World Cup Final the performance of Jack Taylor was as much discussed as the performance of any player. Because of his complete mastery the game was never allowed to go beyond the bounds of hard competitive football. His success was established before the match began. From one's previous knowledge of Jack Taylor one can say that he is a man who produces a first-class performance when he has been spurred both mentally and physically, by careful preparation and encouragement. He is the man for the big occasion and will admit that even at the peak of his career as a football referee he has welcomed the advice and constructive help of others. What is more, he is seen to put it into practice. To sum up, the overall performance of the referee and his two colleagues was of the highest standard and reflected great credit on them, on those who had coached them, and on the role which match officials play in the proper conduct of the game.

Official FIFA World Cup Report on match control

From some of the observations made in this chapter it will be apparent that inconsistencies in match control occur at top level. It is not enough to achieve international referee status. There can never be justification for standing still while the game continues to develop. More enthusiastic and dedicated officials are appearing and are needed to advance the study and practice of modern methods of match control. The official FIFA World Cup Report contains a number of suggestions for further study. Some of the suggestions, reproduced below, could affect referees at all levels of the game.

1   *Deliberate handball*

Uniformity of interpretation of the rules and practice on the field is still the most important problem. Coaches welcomed the statements in the guide [see chapter 11 – World Cup memoranda] that players who catch the ball to prevent the development of an attack will be cautioned.

In the early matches of the tournament, referees immediately produced the yellow card and there was genuine feeling that, in consequence, players would refrain from using this grossly unfair tactic.

In later matches, under the control of more experienced referees, it was regretted that players committing such offences were not cautioned.

2   *Red and yellow card system*

The study group commented on apparent anomalies in the use of cards during the tournament. The problem is one of inconsistency.

After a player has received a caution by the showing of the yellow card, the next cautionary offence by such a player calls for a red card and dismissal from the field. This seems to be a problem. There were several offences by the same player which seemed more severe infringements of the law and yet went unpunished ... When a card is shown for one offence and not for a similar one later on, players, coaches and spectators become critical.

3   *Deliberate holding*

National coaches also agreee that the caution (yellow card) for catching the ball to stop a dangerous attack is justified, but they reason that the deliberate catching hold of a player to stop him from going through in attack is equally deserving of an official caution. The study group endorses this viewpoint.

4   *Physical contact*

Player-to-player contact still presents a problem of interpretation. Referees at this level of the game must be knowledgeable and alert to distinguish between the so-called 'professional' foul, where unfair advantage is sought out of a body-contact incident, and that which is genuine. Players are using their arms and bodies illegally

(Law 12) to check an opponent before the ball is received, as well as when playing it. Many of these unfair acts, if not seen or understood by the referee, arouse bitterness between players and stimulate retaliation.

5   *Wall control*
The study group and national coaches were critical of inconsistency in the control of defensive walls facing free kicks in potential goal-scoring positions. They commented that some referees were able to achieve the required distance between the wall and the ball whereas others signalled the free kick when opponents were only five or six yards from the ball.

6   *Off-side*
It is always understood that deliberate off-side play can defeat itself, in that it leads to marginal decisions as to whether or not the player is off-side at the moment the ball is played. There were criticisms that linesmen flagged for off-side when the player was not off-side the moment the ball was played, though clearly off-side when he received it.

To the above can be added:

7   *Goalkeepers' colours*
On many occasions goalkeepers wore items of strip such as shorts and/or stockings which were not consistent with other players in their teams. These differences are not accidental or simply preferred personal colours. They are intended to gain an advantage, apparently minute but in certain situations decisive, by merging into a dark background or confusing opponents with the referee's uniform.

8   *Penalty kicks*
The statement in chapter 7 that one in three penalty kicks is incorrectly supervised was confirmed in this tournament. More attention is needed to this problem to ensure that the referee does not unfairly influence the result of a match by inefficient supervision.

As a final comment on the performance of the FIFA World Cup officials the FIFA report acknowledged that 'The thirty referees and their four German linesmen colleagues played a large part in ensuring that the 1974 FIFA World Cup was such a sporting success'.

How referees are assessed

How is a referee assessed? Who does the assessing? What criteria decide the manner in which a referee performs his duties? How does a referee progress from junior to international level? These and other basic questions are asked by all recruits to refereeing. The answers will vary according to the country and even the locality in which the referee lives. There is no world standard of assessment for all levels.

The first hurdle is, of course, an examination on the theory of the laws coupled with an eyesight test (colours and distance). It is usual for recruits to be given both written and oral tests, which are not competitive. Certain minimum standards must be achieved in both tests before a candidate is successful. A typical examination report as used by an English county football association is reproduced here.

REPORT ON EXAMINATION

Subject	Law and Number		Points to be covered by examiner	Max. marks	Marks obtained
Section 1	Referees	(5)	Referees' duties	5	
	Linesmen	(6)	Linesmen's duties		
GENERAL KNOWLEDGE	Field of play	(1)	Dimensions of field of play, etc.	5	
	The ball	(2)	Max and min. size of ball, etc.		
	Number of players	(3)	Constitution of team, also matters concerning goalkeeper		
	Players' equipment	(4)	Footwear and dangerous equipment		
	Duration of game	(7)	Period of time to be played, extension of period and stoppages	5	
	The start of play	(8)	The place kick, the toss, temporarily suspensions of play		
	Ball in and out of play	(9)	The ball crossing the line, etc.		
	Method of scoring	(10)	How a goal is scored	5	
	Throw-in	(15)	When to award: how it should be taken		
	Goal kick	(16)	When to award: how it should be taken		
	Corner kick	(17)	When to award: how it should be taken		
			Total	20	

Section 2 OFF-SIDE	Off-side (11)	When a player is off-side When a player is *not* off-side When a player cannot be off-side	10	
		Total	10	
Section 3	Free kick (13)	Difference between direct and in-direct free kicks Properly taken free kicks When to award indirect free kicks When to award direct free kicks	5	
FOULS and MISCONDUCT	Fouls and (12) misconduct	The difference between dangerous play, violent conduct, ungentle-manly conduct When a player should be cautioned or sent off How a player should be cautioned or sent off How to deal with offences *not* being a separate breach of the laws	5	
		Total	10	
Section 4 PENALTY KICK	Penalty kick (14)	When to award a penalty kick Infringements by defending side Infringements by attacking side Extending time for penalty kick	10	
		Total	10	

In this particular case the candidate must achieve a minimum of seventy per cent. in each section and subsection. The report shows the grouping of the laws and the topics of each law on which questions are asked. In some countries, such as South America, additional tests are set to establish literacy. A few countries also insist on a basic medical examination.

The most important aspect of assessing refereeing ability is concerned with performance on the field of play. Certain countries insist on a satisfactory field test before awarding a certificate or licence to officiate in competitive football. In countries where there is a shortage of officials – and most countries suffer this problem to some degree – a field test may not be obligatory until newly qualified referees present themselves for promotion to a higher grade. However, the trend is towards incorporating a field test as a standard requirement before a candidate is allowed to referee junior football games. After initial qualification it is practical performance which determines progress to higher levels, although it has been noted that an increasing number of national football associations require further written and oral tests to be passed before confirming higher gradings. This development is commendable because it ensures that officials who wish to control more important matches keep up-to-date with changes to the laws and official memoranda on the game.

A referee is assessed in some areas by the marks awarded by the clubs he controls. Marks are forwarded to league or competition secretaries and are analysed over a period in order to judge the referee's general competence. This is known as the Club Marking System. While the system has its disadvantages, in that markings sometimes relate more to the success or failure of the club concerned than to the ability of the referee, it is sometimes the only system because independent assessments are not available.

The most desirable system is the use of ex-referees to act as objective observers. In some localities ex-referees who are prepared to devote spare time to assessing are rare, and a combination of club marking plus one or two independent assessments may be the only solution. This is generally the case when referees apply for promotion from their initial grading or classification to the next stage. Some regional football associations or competitions are fortunate enough to be able to call on enough ex-officials to organize an assessing scheme completely independent of club markings. The factors judged by these assessors, together with specimen comments, are reproduced on the following pages. The Assessors' report form of the London Football Association is also reproduced. Although the allocation of marks varies slightly, the questions to be answered by assessors, whether judging referees in junior football or in an international match, are almost identical.

The notes of guidance for FIFA referee inspectors indicate a more important purpose for the reports than assessment of individual performance. They comment on the use of such reports as aids to judging uniformity of interpretation of the laws of the game by *all* referees. FIFA inspectors are also required to 'indicate the personality of the referee, his attitude and conception of the game, as well as his tactical approach'.

........................County .... Football Association

REFEREE REPORT

(*CONFIDENTIAL*)

Name of referee   MR. A. BROWN   (Class 2)
(block capitals)

ROVERS F.C.   *v.*   WANDERERS F.C.

on   SATURDAY .... 19. . . .

League or Competition .... COUNTY SENIOR CUP

Weather conditions   Dry afternoon   *State of ground*   Firm
but humid, no breeze

PART A – GENERAL ASSESSMENT

Result 4-1 (home win)

To be based on answers to the following questions:

Was the game easy or difficult to referee?
Does the referee look and act the part?
Is he completely impartial?
Does he control the game with confidence and efficiency?
Is he right in his decisions?

Maximum 10 marks

General remarks: The game was fairly easy to referee. Mr Brown at times seems to run in an awkward manner but this does not affect his general control of the game. He is impartial and fairly efficient, usually right in his decisions. He is, however, in need of some advice regarding positioning (see Part C) and the use of linesmen where they are qualified officials – neglect of this point may lead him into difficult situations in future matches.

PART B - DETAILED REPORT
Give a brief report on the following factors and also a mark, using the above scale of assessment.

PERSONAL QUALITIES

1   *Appearance (dress, bearing, etc.)*
Good dress; confident in appearance; gave most decisions in a firm, emphatic manner and one which suggested that he would hold his authority in a difficult situation.

2   *Fitness (actual state of fitness; fast, slow; good or poor stamina (etc.)*
Mainly good, but there were two occasions when I thought he took a chance on a clearance being effected when he really ought to have followed the ball through to the goal-line; however, when this is set against his performance for the whole game I would say that he was reasonably fit; he does run a bit awkwardly but he was around the area of play at most times when he gave decisions.

2

3   *Personality (cheerful, anxious, unflurried, panicky, confident, uncertain, quick-thinking, hesitant, modest, showy, etc.)*
Reasonably confident; quick-thinking when giving decisions and applying advantage clause; modest.

3

REFEREEING ABILITY

4   *Impartiality (crowd influence, facing up to difficulties, swayed by result, etc).*
Most certainly impartial. The crowd at this match was fairly quiet so it was hard to judge how the referee would react to a noisy crowd; if anything can be gleaned from the way in which he went through this match it would seem to me that he would be fairly steady under barracking. Did not shirk any issues in this match - free kicks, off sides, etc.

3

5   *Control (attentive to details but afraid of major issues; use of linesmen; clearness of decisions, whistle and signals, etc.)*
He had a weakness in as much as he did not appear to be used to qualified officials as linesmen with the result that he overlooked one off-side decision; also I could not see why he took up a position for corners on the same side of the field as his linesman.

2

6   *Correctness in decisions (technical points and facts of law where referee wrong)*
Apart from the off-side decision which he missed through not checking with his linesman, his decisions were correct.

3

PART C
Suggestions which you think would help referee to improve his efficiency.
Mr Brown could improve his positioning, especially at corner kicks, where it would be better to stand on the other side of the penalty area to his linesman. I suggest he studies *The Referees' Chart* in this connection.

Signed.........J. Smith......

Date.................

London Football Association
Assessor's report

CONFIDENTIAL   FILE NO: REFERENCE:

NAME OF REFEREE _____ CLASS:_____

MATCH AND RESULT _____ v _____

COMPETITION _____DIVN./ROUND IF CUP_____

DATE OF MATCH _____GROUND AND WEATHER_____

EASY/DIFFICULT MATCH – OBSERVATIONS
ADEQUATE/INADEQUATE TEST OF ABILITY

ASSESSMENT
   Section 1
   General control:
____ Marks out of 5 (a)   Did he face up to difficulties? Was he influenced by the crowd?
____ Marks out of 5 (b)   Were his decisions given clearly?
____ Marks out of 5 (c)   Did he make effective use of his linesmen?
____ Marks out of 5 (d)   Was his positioning satisfactory?

Section 2

Application of laws:

____ Marks out of 5   Was the referee generally correct in his decisions based on your interpretation of the laws of the game? (NB Isolated controversial decisions must be ignored.)

Section 3

Personality and appearance:

____ Marks out of 5 (a)   Was the referee confident and quick-thinking?

____ Marks out of 5 (b)   Did his appearance and personality inspire con-fidence?

I award the referee a total of   marks out of 10 for the manner in which he controlled the above match.

NB This mark reflects overall performance and should not be arrived at by averaging marks on left-hand side.

Specific comments against each section would be of great assistance to note for advice to referee at a later date should he fail in his bid for promotion.

GENERAL REMARKS ON THE REFEREE: _____

_____

_____

_____

_____(Continue overleaf if necessary.)

LINESMEN   OFFICIAL/CLUB/NONE (delete as applicable)

GENERAL REMARKS ON THE LINESMEN: _____

_____

_____

_____

Did the referee approach you after the match? YES/NO

If so, did you give him any information? YES/NO

Would you recommend the referee for promotion on this performance? YES/NO

Report submitted by: _____

Assessor No.

It is, of course, important that any authority responsible for the appointment of referees should have information on the competence of all officials. It is equally important that, where possible, the flow of information should be two-way, that is, individual referees should be given advice on which aspects of their performance need improvement. If this is not done referees will be ignorant of their deficiencies and will continue bad habits throughout their careers to the detriment not only of themselves but of the game in general.

Some assessment forms do provide for comments for the benefit of the referee. The assessing system employed by the Football League incorporates detailed questions for the assessor which act as a checklist of standard requirements. In addition comments are invited on faults noted and constructive suggestions for improvement. The system employs about eighty assessors, and referees are assessed at every match. Copies of assessors' reports are forwarded to referees so that a clear picture of performance can be formulated and particular problem areas highlighted.

Finally, the assessment of referees is of as much importance to the welfare of the game as the refereeing itself. Assessors are nearly all ex-referees with considerable experience. The fact that they continue to give service after retirement speaks volumes for their devotion to the game.

Summary

The standard of refereeing throughout the world must be set by those officials who operate at top level. Their actions are seen by millions of football followers and by many thousands of referee colleagues. It is appropriate therefore that the first section of this chapter should concentrate on the performances of top-level referees engaged in the FIFA World Cup tournament. As has been observed, while the overall standard contributed towards the success of the 1974 tournament, there are areas of technique and interpretation on which further work is needed. This fact suggests that the need to achieve uniformity of interpretation and application at other levels is even more pressing.

One point of particular moment, highlighted by its dramatic effect on the choice of referee to control the World Cup Final, is the vital role of linesmen in helping the referee to provide total control of the field. It may be of some consolation to Bob Davidson to know that his personal misfortune has directed more attention to off-the-ball situations and may have saved the final match from an ugly incident. The standard of cooperation between referee and linesmen throughout the world will be better for the spotlight of criticism being focused on his one oversight during the Holland *v.* Brazil match. World Cup Final tournaments provide excellent study opportunities for new and experienced referees. From points covered in this book, from the detailed information published before each tournament, by viewing many games on film and television, and through his knowledge of the official assessing criteria, the reader can judge the individual and collective standards of performance in future series. His or her own performance on the field of play must surely benefit from such studies.

$\underset{\text{13}}{\text{13}}$ Match Problems

Off-side situations

No. 8 shoots for goal. The ball rebounds from the crossbar to No. 11. Although No. 11 was behind the ball when it hit the crossbar he was off-side the moment No. 8 played the ball, not having two opponents nearer the goal-line. It is the equivalent of a direct pass.

The ball is kicked into goal but No. 7, in an off-side position, would be judged to be interfering with play by obstructing or distracting the goalkeeper. The goal would not be allowed.

Not off-side

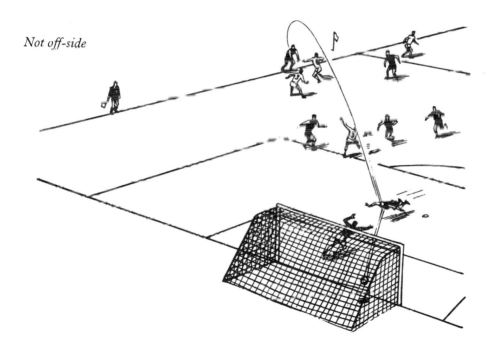

A player cannot be off-side if he receives the ball from a throw-in. The goal would be allowed.

P

Not off-side

No. 7 has run on to the ball from a forward pass. No. 7 was not in front of the ball when last played by his team-mate; he is therefore not off-side.

Match problems

The following pages represent a small selection of problems which have been illustrated in a regular feature of the weekly Soccer magazine, *Shoot*, published by IPC Magazines Ltd. London. The feature informs readers on the practical application of the laws of the game.

1 From a goal-kick the ball is passed to a defender inside the penalty-area. He kicks it back to his goalkeeper but the ball goes into the goal. Do you (a) award a goal, (b) a free-kick or (c) have the goal kick retaken?

2 An attacker wants to take a penalty - kick quickly when two defenders have not left the penalty-area and the goalkeeper is not on the goal-line. Do you (a) delay the signal until the defenders are in position or (b) signal and have the penalty retaken if a goal is not scored?

3 A player removes a corner-post to obtain more space to take a corner-kick. Do you (a) take no action or (b) have the post replaced before the kick is taken?

4 At a kick-off an attacker runs into the opponents' half before the ball is kicked. You stop play and award a free-kick where the attacker encroached.

From the free-kick the ball goes direct to a player of the same team when he is in an offside position. You award a free-kick. (Where is the problem?)

ANSWERS

1. The goal-kick must be retaken (c) because the ball did not go into play beyond the penalty-area. 2. The signal should be delayed (a) until all players are correctly positioned. 3. The corner-post must be replaced (b) before the corner-kick is taken. 4. The problem is in A. The free-kick award is incorrect. The kick-off should be retaken after the attacker has returned to his own half. In B there is no problem. A player can be offside from a free-kick.

1 Time runs out as you are about to drop the ball immediately in front of goal. Should you (a) signal the end of the match or (b) extend time to complete the drop-ball?

2 When inspecting the pitch you notice the flagposts are missing from the halfway line. Do you (a) refuse to start until the posts are obtained, (b) start but report the matter or (c) take no action?

3 When the ball is in play, near the centre-circle, a defender runs over the goal-line, from his penalty-area, and strikes a spectator. After stopping play to dismiss the defender do you re-start with (a) a penalty-kick, (b) a direct free-kick or (c) a drop-ball where the ball was?

4

A: An attacker prevents a goalkeeper from releasing the ball by jumping up and down in front of the 'keeper. You stop play, caution the attacker and award an indirect free-kick.

B: Before the free-kick can be taken the goalkeeper strikes the attacker. You dismiss the 'keeper and award a penalty-kick. *(Where is the problem?)*

ANSWERS

1. Signal the end of the match (a). Time can only be extended for a penalty-kick. 2. Take no action (c) because the flagposts on the halfway line are optional equipment. 3. Play must be restarted with a drop-ball (c) because the offence occurred off the pitch. 4. The problem is in B. The penalty award is incorrect because the ball was not in play when the goalkeeper struck the attacker. In A the action taken is correct.

1 An attacker (number 9) lines up with defenders, on the goal-line between the goal-posts, to face an indirect free-kick less than ten yards from goal. After the ball is kicked he steps forward out of the wall, and the ball goes through the gap into goal. Do you (a) award a goal, (b) a goal-kick or (c) a free-kick to the defending team?

2 When taking a throw-in a player stands with both feet on the touch-line. Do you (a) take no action, (b) have the throw retaken or (c) award a throw-in to the other team?

3 A goalkeeper falls to the ground, injured, immediately before the ball is kicked into the goal. Do you (a) award a goal, (b) a goal-kick or (c) drop the ball?

4 A: Receiving the ball from a throw-in an attacker passes the ball forward to a team-mate who is in an offside position outside the penalty-area. He scores but you disallow the goal and award a free-kick

B: The free-kick is taken quickly by a defender. The ball strikes your back and rebounds over the goalkeeper's head into the goal. You award a goal.

(Where is the problem?)

ANSWERS

1. Award a free-kick (c). The attacker was offside when the ball was kicked, not having at least two defenders between himself and the goal-line. 2. "...part of each foot shall be either on the touch-line or on the ground outside the touchline." 3. Award a goal (a). 4. The problem is in B. The correct decision is a corner-kick because a defender cannot score against his own team from a free-kick.

1 An attacker scores with an overhead kick when the ball is about to be headed by a defender. Should you (a) award a goal (b) a direct free-kick against the attacker or (c) an indirect free-kick against him?

3 When the ball enters the goalmouth the goalkeeper attempts to punch it. He misses but strikes an opponent. Do you (a) take no action (b) award a penalty-kick or (c) an indirect free-kick for dangerous play?

2 At a kick-off a player kicks the ball backwards and then plays it again. Do you (a) take no action (b) have the kick-off retaken or (c) award a free-kick?

4 A: The ball is kicked towards the touch line. It strikes a spectator, who is standing on the touch-line, and rebounds into play. An attacker gains possesssion and shoots towards the goal.

B: A defender stops the ball with his hand, when standing inside the penalty-arc. You award a free-kick to the attackers instead of a penalty-kick. (Where is the problem?)

ANSWERS

1. An overhead-kick, attempted when opponents are close to the ball, is a dangerous act and should be penalised by an indirect free-kick (c). 2. The ball was not kicked forward and was not in play when the player kicked it for the second time. The kick-off should be retaken (b). 3. Take no action (a) if you are satisfied that the goalkeeper intended to punch the ball and not the opponent. 4. The problem is in A. When the ball struck the spectator, play should be stopped and restarted with a drop-ball. In B the free-kick, outside the penalty-area, is correct because the penalty-arc is not part of the penalty-area.

Bibliography

In chapter 8 the reader is recommended to keep a personal library of publications relating to various aspects of football. To help him in his selection of suitable works the following list includes several official guides and books by individuals which the author has found valuable. Several of these works have influenced this book. The author is pleased to record his sincere appreciation to the authorities and individuals concerned.

Official publications

The following publications and films are available from FIFA, most in several languages (E = English, F = French, S = Spanish, D = German).

1 *FIFA Handbook 1977/78* (E, F, S, D)
2 *Laws of the Game and Universal Guide for Referees* (E, F, S, D)
3 *Handbook for Referee Instructors* (E, F, S)
4 *Signals by the Referee and Linesman* (E, F, S, D)
5 *Technical Study:*
  World Championships 1966 (E) *and 1970* (E, F, S)
  1974 FIFA World Cup (E, F, S, D)
6 *World Cup Report 1970* (E)
7 *World Cup Report 1974* (E, F, S, D)
8 *History of the Laws of the Game* (E), Sir Stanley Rous and Donald Ford
9 *Association Football Laws Illustrated* (F, S), Stanley Lover. The English edition is published by Pelham Books, London.

Films

1 *Allowed or Forbidden* – West German FA film on Law 12 (FIFA commentary in English, black and white, 16mm, length 342m.)

2 *Four-Step Rule for Goalkeepers* – FIFA film (English commentary, colour, 16mm, length 125m.)
3 *Law XII – Incidents* – FIFA film on Law 12 (English commentary, black and white, 16mm, length 246m.)
4 *Referee and Linesmen – A Team* – diagonal system of control and positioning of referees (English commentary, colour, 16mm, length 235m.)
5 *Swiss test film for referees* (no commentary, 70 scenes, black and white, 16mm, length 213m.)
6 *Towards Uniformity of Interpretation* – FIFA film (English commentary, colour, 16mm, length 290m.)

Current prices and forwarding charges may be obtained from the Federation Internationale de Football Association, FIFA House, 11 Hitzigweg, 8032 Zurich, Switzerland.

The following publications are available from The Football Association, 16 Lancaster Gate, London W2 3LW:

1   *FA Guide for Referees and Linesmen*
2   *FA Guide to the Laws of the Game*
3   *FA Guide to Training and Coaching*
4   *Know the Game Association Football* (E.P. Publications, Leeds)
5   *Referees' Chart and the Laws of the Game*
6   *Referees' Quiz Book*
7   *Tactics and Teamwork*

Other Publications

Norman BURTENSHAW, *Whose side are you on, Ref?* Arthur Barker, London.
HARRIS & HARRIS, *Fair or Foul?*, Soccer for Americans, California.
Denis HOWELL, *Soccer Refereeing*, Pelham Books, London.
Eric SELLIN, *The Inner Game of Soccer*, World Publications, Croydon.
Jack TAYLOR, *World Soccer Referee*, Pelham Books, London.
Martin TYLER, *The Story of Football*, Marshall Cavendish Publications, London.

FIFA World Cup 1974

Referees selected

Luis Pestarino
Argentina

Tony Boskovic
Australia

Linemayr
ria

Vital Loraux
Belgium

Armando Marques
Brazil

Werner Winsemann
Canada

Delgado
bia

Mostafa Kamel
Egypt

John Taylor
England

Rudi Glöckner
German DR

Kurt Tschenscher
Germany FR

Hans-Joachim Weyland
Germany FR

Kurt Schulenburg
Germany FR

Karoly Palotai
Hungary

Jafar Namdar
Iran

Aurelio Angonese
Italy

Alfonso Gonzales Archundia
Mexico

Arie van Gemert
Netherlands

Edison Perez Nuñez
Peru

Nicolae Rainea
Rumania

Robert Davidson
Scotland

Youssou N'Diaye
Senegal

ndasamy Suppiah
pore

Pablo Sanchez Ibañez
Spain

Rudolf Scheurer
Switzerland

Dogan Babacan
Turkey

n Barreto Ruiz
uay

Pavel Kasakov
USSR

Vicente Llobregat
Venezuela

Clive Thomas
Wales

Aldinger
any FR

Ferdinand Biwersi
Germany FR

Walter Eschweiler
Germany FR

Klaus Ohmsen
Germany FR

Details of Referees selected

Country and Nationality	Surname	Christian Name(s)	Date of Birth	Profession	Home Town	Mother Tongue	Other Languages Spoken	Height cm	Internat. Matches "A"	Others
Argentina	Pestarino	Luis	28. 5.28	Employee	Buenos Aires	Spanish	–	186	13	1
Australia	Boskovic	Tony	27. 1.33	Salesman	Fairfield	Yugoslav	English Russian Italian German	169	10	–
Austria	Linemayr	Erich	24. 1.33	Clerk	Linz	German	English	180	7	6
Belgium	Loraux	Vital	22. 9.25	Management Officer	Montignies-le-Tilleul	French	–	180	14	6
Brazil	Marques	Armando	6. 2.30	Tradesman	Rio de Janeiro	Portuguese	Spanish French English	175	20	6
Canada	Winsemann	Werner	15. 1.33	Auto Body Repairs	Vancouver	German	English	182	6	–
Colombia	Delgado	Omar	21. 1.41	Sports Teacher	Medellín	Spanish	English	181	3	6
Egypt AR	Mahmoud	Mostafa Kamel	7.11.27	Employer	Cairo	English	–	184	7	1
England	Taylor	John Keith	21. 5.30	Butcher	Wolverhampton	English	–	185,5	21	6
German DR	Glöckner	Rudi	20. 3.29	Tradesman	Markranstädt	German	English	183	17	4
Germany FR	Schulenburg	Gerhard	11.10.26	Clerk	Laatzen-Grasdorf	German	English	176	16	2
Germany FR	Tschenscher	Kurt	5.10.28	Local government officer	Mannheim	German	English	179	40	1
Germany FR	Weyland	Hans-Joachim	29. 9.29	Personnel officer	Oberhausen	German	English	192	4	6
Hungary	Palotai	Károly	11. 9.35	Clerk	Györ	Hungarian	German	184	2	–
Iran	Namdar	Jafar	2. 7.34	Manager	Tehran	English	–	170	5	8

Country	Surname	First name	Date of birth	Occupation	City	Language 1	Language 2	Height		
Netherlands	Van Gemert	Arie	23. 3.29	Computer Operator	Dordrecht	Dutch	English German	182	4	4
Peru	Perez Nuñez	Edison	14. 4.36	Clerk	Lima	Spanish	Portuguese English	174	6	–
Rumania	Rainea	Nicolae	19.11.33	Head Foreman	Birland	Rumanian	–	179	2	2
Scotland	Davidson	Robert Holley	19. 7.28	Managing Director	Airdrie	English	German	185	26	–
Senegal	N'Diaye	Youssoupha	20. 6.32	Draughts-man	Dakar	French	–	185	6	–
Singapore	Suppiah	Govindasamy	17. 6.29	Sports Teacher	Singapore	Tamil	English	160	28	1
Spain	Sanchez Ibañez	Pablo Augusto	25. 1.30	Information Officer	Badajoz	Spanish	French	180	3	–
Switzerland	Scheurer	Rudolf	25. 5.25	Teacher	Bettlach	German	French English	192	20	1
Turkey	Babacan	Dogan	5. 4.30	Tradesman	Istanbu	Turkish	English	170	6	1
Uruguay	Barreto	Ramón	14. 9.37	Tradesman	Montevideo	Spanish	English	185	11	2
USSR	Kazakov	Pavel	19. 2.28	Football Teacher	Moscow	Russian	German	176	6	–
Venezuela	Llobregat Vicedo	Vicente	28.10.32	Bookkeeper	Caracas	Spanish	–	172	2	–
Wales	Thomas	Clive	27. 6.36	General Secretary	Glamorgan	English	–	172	2	1
Germany FR (Selected as linesmen)	Aldinger	Heinz	7. 1.33	Brewer's Represent-ative	Waiblingen b. Stuttgart	German	English	172	1	2
	Biwersi	Ferdinand	24. 6.34	Security official	Bliesransbach	German	–	181	10	1
	Eschweiler	Walter	20. 9.35	Civil servant	Bonn-Duisdorf	German	English French	188	2	13
	Ohmsen	Klaus	16.10.35	Head of depart-ment	Hamburg	German	–	183	1	1

Index